TWELVE TRIBES OF ISRAEL

Activity Book

Bible Pathway
Adventures

DEFENDERS OF THE FAITH

Twelve Tribes of Israel Activity Book

Bible Pathway Adventures® is a trademark of BPA Publishing Ltd.
Defenders of the Faith® is a trademark of BPA Publishing Ltd.

ISBN: 978-1-989961-74-2

Author: Pip Reid
Creative Director: Curtis Reid

For more Bible resources, including Activity Books and printables, visit our website at:

www.biblepathwayadventures.com

◦◇ **Introduction** ◇◦

Step into an adventure that began thousands of years ago! This Twelve Tribes of Israel Activity Book takes you on a journey through the history of the twelve tribes of Israel, from Jacob (also called Israel) and his twelve sons, to when the Israelites entered the Promised Land. Along the way, you'll meet shepherds and rulers, travel through deserts and rivers, witness mighty miracles, and learn how Yah shaped His people into a great nation.

Through engaging worksheets, maps, coloring pages, puzzles, and Bible quizzes, you'll explore the lives of the tribes one step at a time. We'll follow their story in the order it happened, starting in the land of Canaan, traveling down to Egypt with Joseph, escaping slavery under Moses, receiving the covenant at Mount Sinai, and finally crossing the Jordan River with Joshua.

Packed with Scripture references, historical insights, and hands-on activities, this book will help you discover how each tribe had a unique role in Israel's history. Whether you're at home, in a classroom, or part of a study group, you'll gain a deeper understanding of the Bible while having fun learning. Bible Pathway Adventures® helps educators teach children a Biblical faith in a fun and engaging way. We do this via our Activity Books and printable activities – all available on our website: www.biblepathwayadventures.com

The search for Truth is more fun than Tradition!

◇◈ Table of Contents ◈◇

The Tabernacle and the wilderness

Joshua and the Promised Land

12 tribes of Israel worksheets

Crafts and projects

Jacob and his family

YOUR ISRAELITE ADVENTURE BEGINS!

 **Step 1:**

A long time ago in the land of Canaan, there lived a Hebrew leader named Jacob. He had two wives, Leah and Rachel, and two concubines, Bilhah and Zilpah. Together they had twelve sons: Reuben, Simeon, Levi, Judah, Dan, Naphtali, Gad, Asher, Issachar, Zebulun, Joseph, and Benjamin. They also had at least one daughter named Dinah. The descendants of these twelve sons became the twelve tribes of Israel (Genesis 49).

Each tribe was named after a son or grandson of Jacob (also called Israel). Even though the tribes formed one nation, each tribe was different. In fact, Jacob gave each of his sons a unique blessing before he died (Genesis 49).

 **Step 2:**

Many years later, after the Hebrews had been slaves in Egypt, Yah chose a man named Moses to lead them out of Egypt and back to the land of Canaan - the Promised Land. On their journey, the Hebrews became the great nation of Israel. And together, they had many adventures.

 **Did You Know?**

Yah changed Jacob's name to Israel after he wrestled with an angel of God (Genesis 32:28). Israel means "to wrestle with Yah and men, and overcome."

Who was Jacob?

Read Genesis 25:19-33:20 and 35:1-29. Complete the worksheet below.

Isaac sent Jacob to Paddan-aram because:

....

Describe Jacob's dream:

....

Jacob worked for:

....

Jacob had 12 .... named ....

....

....

Jacob is most famous for:

....

....

Five words that describe Jacob:

1. ....

2. ....

3. ....

4. ....

5. ....

Read Genesis 32:22-32. Retell the story of Jacob wresting with the stranger in your own words.

"Your name shall no longer be called Jacob, but Israel."

(Genesis 32:28)

Jacob becomes ISRAEL

Read Genesis 32:22-32. Find and circle the words below.

```
G T W M Z H C N N J W T C N U
A W A R O B G R Z V R E J C X
U J A J E Y T X D G T F A W R
P Y A S I S J Y W Y L L B I O
G R U C J S T S A L E H B S U
R Y E V O J R L N Y B I O H W
C Z X V D B L A E P C P K I Q
L Y W U A F S N E Z X S I S S
U F L T I I U K G L D O V L E
Z Z W N L K L G G B C C W I G
R J U Y R O Q K C Z Z K V M I
Y S T R I V E N M X Z E V P H
M E N F H I O Z B E F T A C V
Q I Q F V I P E N I E L W J H
S G O D Q A E N A M E O L H X
```

WRESTLE

JACOB

HIP SOCKET

PREVAIL

NAME

LIMP

JABBOK

MEN

PENIEL

ISRAEL

GOD

STRIVEN

Family of JACOB

Jacob had two wives - Leah and Rachel - and two concubines, Bilhah and Zilpah. Together, they had twelve sons. Read Genesis 29–30, 35 and write the names of their sons in the correct column below.

LEAH	RACHEL	ZILPAH	BILHAH
......	......	......	......
......	......	......	......
......	......	......	......
......	......	......	......
......	......	......	......

Bible Pathway Adventures
JACOB'S FAMILY

Read Genesis 29–30 and 35:16–18.
Write one son's name below each portrait, then answer the questions.

....

....

Discussion questions:

1. Why do you think Jacob had such a large family?

2. What are some challenges you think Jacob's family might have faced?

3. Why is Jacob's family important in the Bible?

www.biblepathwayadventures.com
Twelve Tribes of Israel Activity Book
© BPA Publishing Ltd 2022

Joseph's journey

Joseph the DREAMER

Read Genesis 37:1-11. Answer the questions below.

1. Where did Jacob (Israel) live?

2. How old was Joseph when he was pasturing the flock with his brothers?

3. Who were the sons that Joseph was with when pasturing the flock?

4. Why did Israel (Jacob) love Joseph more than his other sons?

5. What special gift did Jacob give to Joseph?

6. How did Joseph's brothers feel when they saw that their father loved him more?

7. What did Joseph see in his first dream?

8. How did Joseph's brothers react to his first dream?

9. What did Joseph see in his second dream?

10. How did Jacob react when Joseph told him the second dream?

"I dreamed another dream. The sun, the moon, and eleven stars bowed down to me."

(Genesis 37:9)

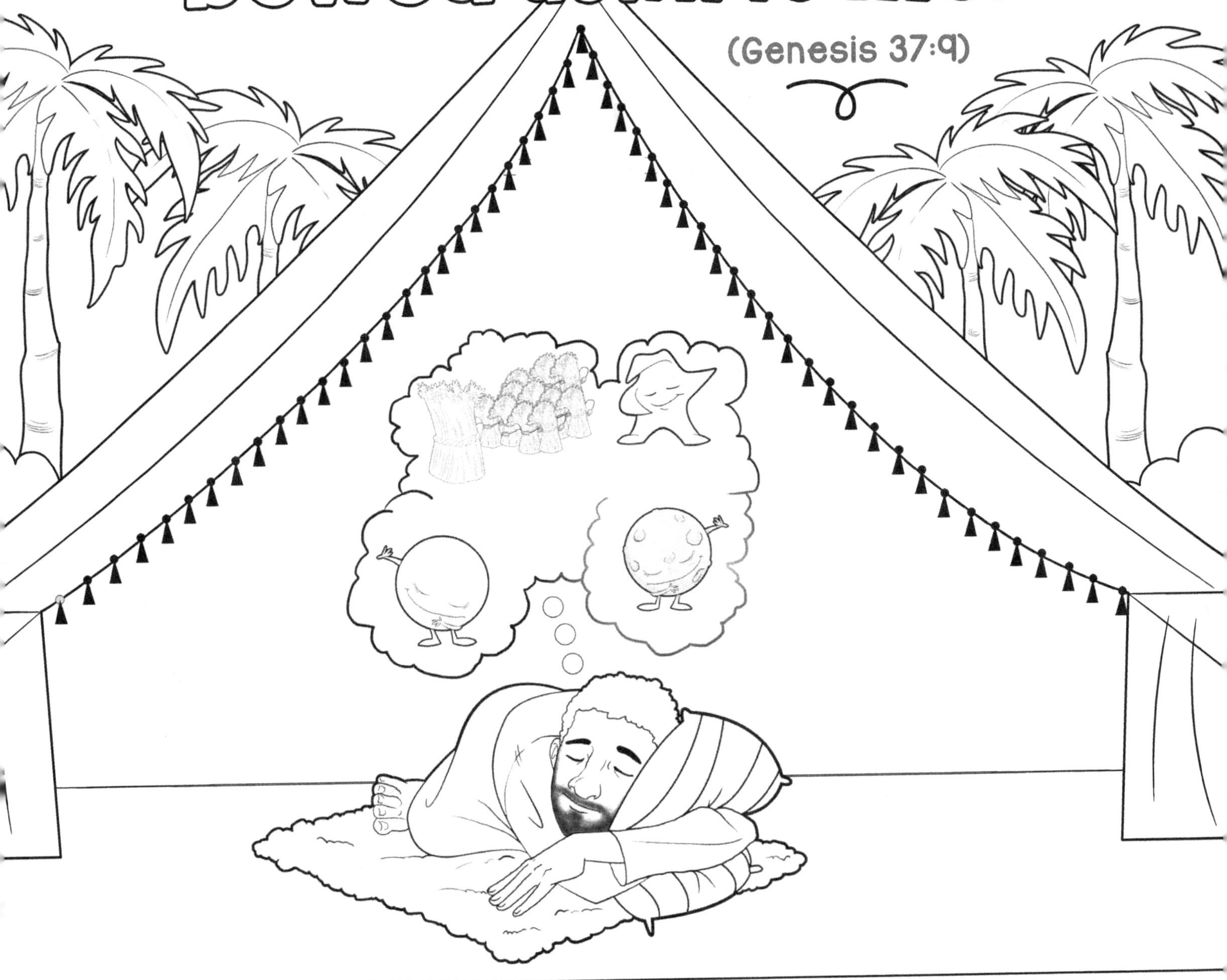

Duties of a shepherd

At the time of the patriarchs (Abraham, Isaac, and Jacob), it was common to care for animals like sheep and goats. Sheep were used for their milk, meat, and wool, and being a shepherd was seen as an important job. The sons of Isaac and Jacob were all shepherds (Genesis 30:29; 37:12). But a shepherd's life was not easy.

Shepherds spent most of their time outside with their animals, no matter what the weather was like. To protect their flocks from wild animals and thieves, shepherds often slept nearby. In the spring, sheep stayed near the village or camp to eat grass. After farmers harvested their grain, shepherds let their flocks eat leftover plants. When that food was gone, they took the animals into the open fields to graze.

At night, shepherds brought their sheep into 'sheepfolds' - safe places made from stone walls or natural spots like caves. Each evening, they used a rod to count the animals as they entered, and again in the morning when they left for the fields. Some flocks had as many as 1,000 sheep and goats! Later, when Jacob's sons moved to Egypt, they found a different way of life. The Egyptians were farmers and did not like shepherds. They thought sheep ruined their crops and were not useful for food or sacrifices.

I. Why was being a shepherd considered an important job in Bible times?

....

....

2. How did shepherds protect their flocks from danger at night?

....

....

3. Why did the Egyptians dislike shepherds and sheep?

....

....

Book of Genesis

The
Canaan Chronicle

GENESIS 37 | LAND OF CANAAN | A BIBLE HISTORY PUBLICATION

Shepherds behave badly

....

....

....

....

....

....

Wolves seen near camp

Family feud!

....

....

....

....

Sold into SLAVERY

Read Genesis 37:12-24. Answer the questions below.

1. Where did Joseph's brothers go to take care of their father's sheep?

2. Who sent Joseph to check on his brothers?

3. When Joseph arrived in Shechem, where did he learn his brothers had gone?

4. What did Joseph's brothers plan to do when they saw him coming from a distance?

5. Which brother suggested they throw Joseph into a pit instead of killing him?

6. What did the brothers take from Joseph before throwing him into the pit?

7. Was the pit that Joseph was thrown into full of water?

8. What did the brothers decide to do with Joseph instead of killing him?

9. How much silver did the brothers receive for selling Joseph?

10. Who bought Joseph from the traders when they arrived in Egypt?

"Joseph's brothers threw him into a pit."

(Genesis 37:24)

Journey to Egypt

Joseph's brothers sold him into slavery (Genesis 37:28). Connect the dots to trace Joseph's journey from Canaan to the land of Egypt. Then, imagine you are Joseph. Write a letter to your father, Jacob (Israel), explaining what happened on the journey.

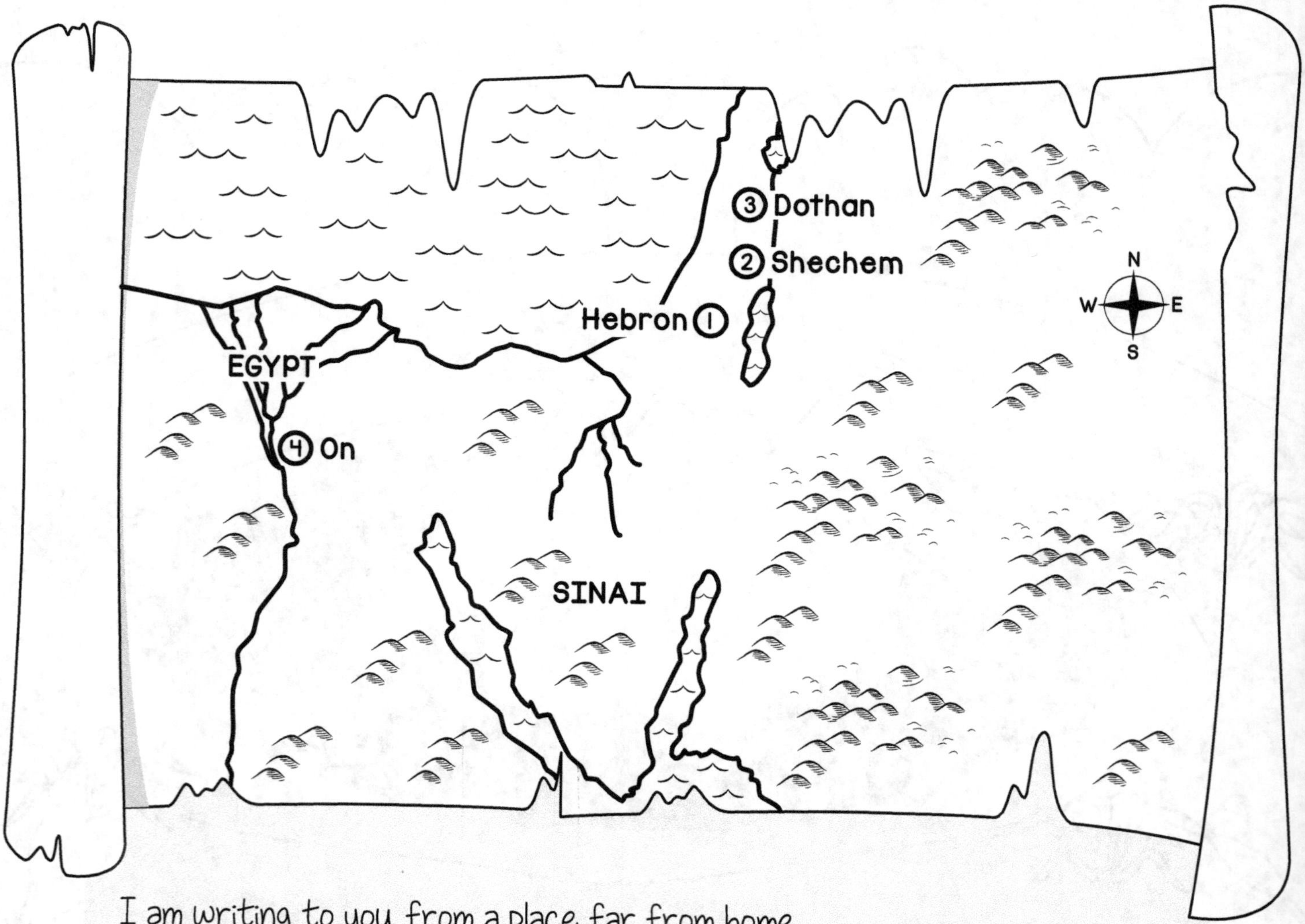

③ Dothan
② Shechem
Hebron ①

EGYPT
④ On

SINAI

N W E S

I am writing to you from a place far from home... ....

....

....

....

....

Design your own silver coin

Silver was often used as money in the ancient Middle East. The first coins were made in a place called Lydia. These coins were made from a mix of gold and silver called electrum. The government stamped the coins to show they were real and to mark their value. Later, people across the Middle East and Asia used silver coins to trade and buy things. In the Bible, Midianite traders bought Joseph for 20 silver coins (Genesis 37:28). They took him to Egypt and sold him as a slave to Potiphar, one of Pharaoh's officials.

Design both sides of your
coin in the spaces below.
Use your imagination!

Color the
trader!

Match the characters

Below are descriptions of actions from the story of Joseph working for Potiphar.
Read Genesis 39:1-23 carefully. Then, match each description with the correct
Bible character: Joseph, Potiphar, or Potiphar's wife, by drawing a line.

Joseph

Potiphar

Potiphar's wife

Trusted Joseph and made him the overseer of his house.

Ran away when tempted to do something wrong.

Noticed that Joseph was handsome.

Was successful in everything he did because God was with him.

Got angry when he believed a lie and put someone in prison.

Told a lie that caused someone else to get into trouble.

Blessed by God because of Joseph's presence.

Was put in charge of everything, both in the house and in the field.

Why is it important to tell the truth, and how did Joseph show integrity?

"Joseph said to them, "Do not interpretations belong to God? Please tell me your dreams." "

(Genesis 40:8)

Pharaoh's dreams

Pharaoh, the king of Egypt, had two dreams that he did not understand. He called for Joseph to help explain them. Read Genesis 41:1–36 and write Pharaoh's two dreams below.

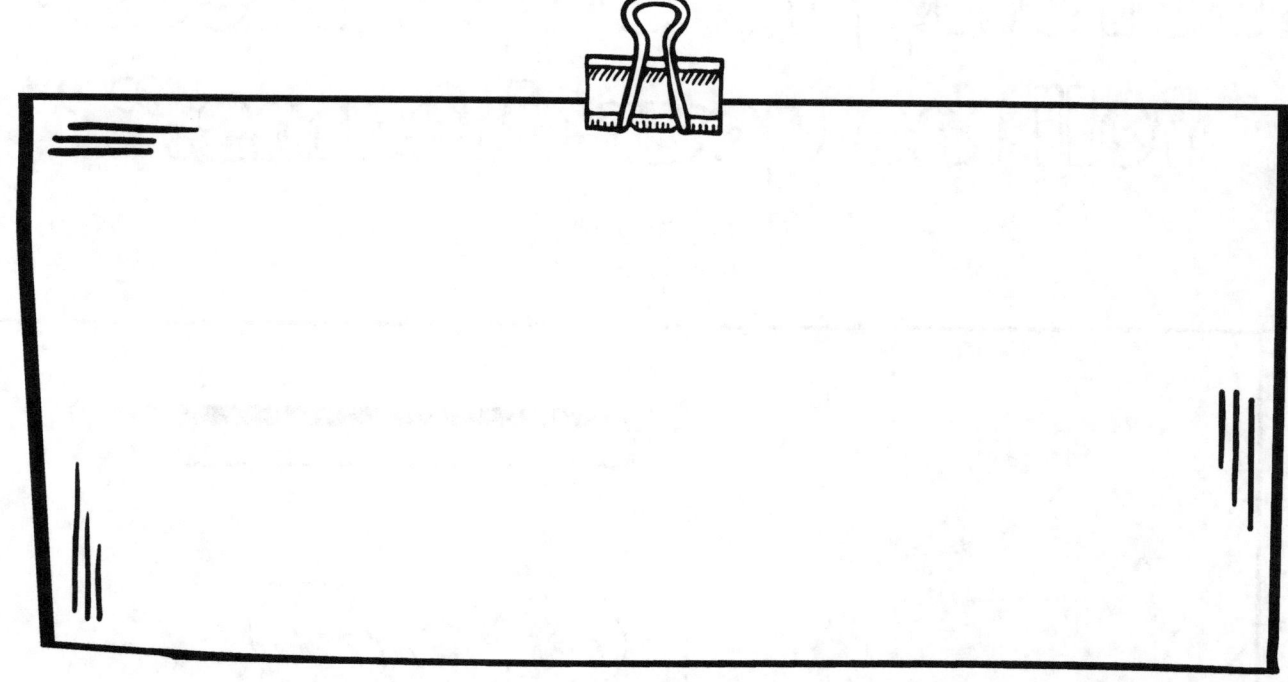

Answer the questions below.

Who could not explain the meaning of Pharaoh's dreams?

Who told Pharaoh about Joseph?

What did Joseph tell Pharaoh to do?

Pharaoh's DREAMS

Read Genesis 41:1-52. Find and circle the words below.

```
G F A M I N E A U E J T M Z E
O K A S P P F H Z G O O A T A
X K D W A W D V A Y S U U A M
D J D P V K Q V I P E H T Y N
R S X Y X E B Z P T P O H Q M
G Y P S I G P T J X H H O D W
O R H Q E I B H H T L U R G M
C U A S M V Q X J R T X I Z H
Z P R I W W E D F U Z D T G U
E B A X N I E N J I L D Y P N
K M O N R I V E R B A N K S G
Z X H K D E C O L S W L P Q E
D R E A M R I K Z R O B Q M R
P L E N T Y C Y G X O L T N D
G M N Y W I S E M E N Q T N H
```

GRAIN

EGYPT

SEVEN

RIVERBANK

PHARAOH

AUTHORITY

JOSEPH

HUNGER

DREAM

PLENTY

FAMINE

WISE MEN

Because Joseph helped Pharaoh understand his two dreams, he rose to power in Egypt. Unscramble the words to learn how Pharaoh rewarded Joseph.

JOSEPH!

nestig nrgi ....

ifen eninl ....

odgl inhac ....

irctaho ....

fwei ....

trsngema ....

rragamie ....

tEpgy ....

✳ Read the story of Joseph's rise to power in Genesis 41:37-45 (ESV).

Draw and Write
Joseph stores food

For seven years, Joseph prepared for the famine. He collected food during the years of plenty and stored it in cities across Egypt. Joseph made sure there was enough grain to feed the people when the famine came. Read Genesis 41:1-57 and answer the questions below.

FAMINE

1 Why did Joseph prepare for the famine?

....

....

2 How did Joseph organize the storage of grain to keep it safe?

....

....

3 After the famine started, what did Joseph do for the Egyptians and the foreigners?

....

....

Pharaoh's storehouses

During the years of plenty, the Egyptians were required to give 1/5th of their grain to Pharaoh's storehouses.

"Let Pharaoh proceed to appoint overseers over the land and take one-fifth of the produce of the land of Egypt during the seven plentiful years. And let them gather all the food of these good years that are coming and store up grain under the authority of Pharaoh for food in the cities, and let them keep it." (Genesis 41:34-35)

Why do you think Pharaoh did this?

Solve the equations:

To find 1/5th of a number, divide by five!

1/5th of 20 =

1/5th of 50 =

1/5th of 140 =

1/5th of 265 =

1/5th of 360 =

1/5th of 700 =

1/5th of 1650 =

1/5th of 2000 =

The search for grain!

Read Genesis 42:1-11 (ESV). Using the words below,
fill in the blanks to complete the Bible passage.

JACOB	BROTHERS	DREAMS	CANAAN	GOVERNOR	GRAIN
EGYPT	JOSEPH	FAMINE	SERVANTS	STRANGERS	SPIES

66 When .... learned that there was grain for sale in Egypt, he said to his sons, "Why do you look at one another?" And he said, "Behold, I have heard that there is grain for sale in Egypt. Go down and buy .... for us there, that we may live and not die." So ten of Joseph's brothers went down to buy grain in .... But Jacob did not send Benjamin, Joseph's brother, with his brothers, for he feared that harm might happen to him. Thus, the sons of Israel came to buy among the others who came, for the .... was in the land of .... Now Joseph was .... over the land. He was the one who sold to all the people of the land. And Joseph's brothers came and bowed themselves before him with their faces to the ground. Joseph saw his .... and recognized them, but he treated them like .... and spoke roughly to them. "Where do you come from?" he said. They said, "From the land of Canaan, to buy food." And Joseph recognized his brothers, but they did not recognize him. And .... remembered the .... that he had dreamed of them. And he said to them, "You are ....; you have come to see the nakedness of the land." They said to him, "No, my lord, your servants have come to buy food. We are all sons of one man. We are honest men. Your .... have never been spies." 99

Journeys to Egypt

There was a famine in the land of Canaan, so Joseph's brothers went to Egypt to buy grain (Genesis 42:1–5). On the map below, label Egypt, Canaan, and Mesopotamia. Then draw arrows to show how people from different places traveled to Egypt to buy food during the famine.

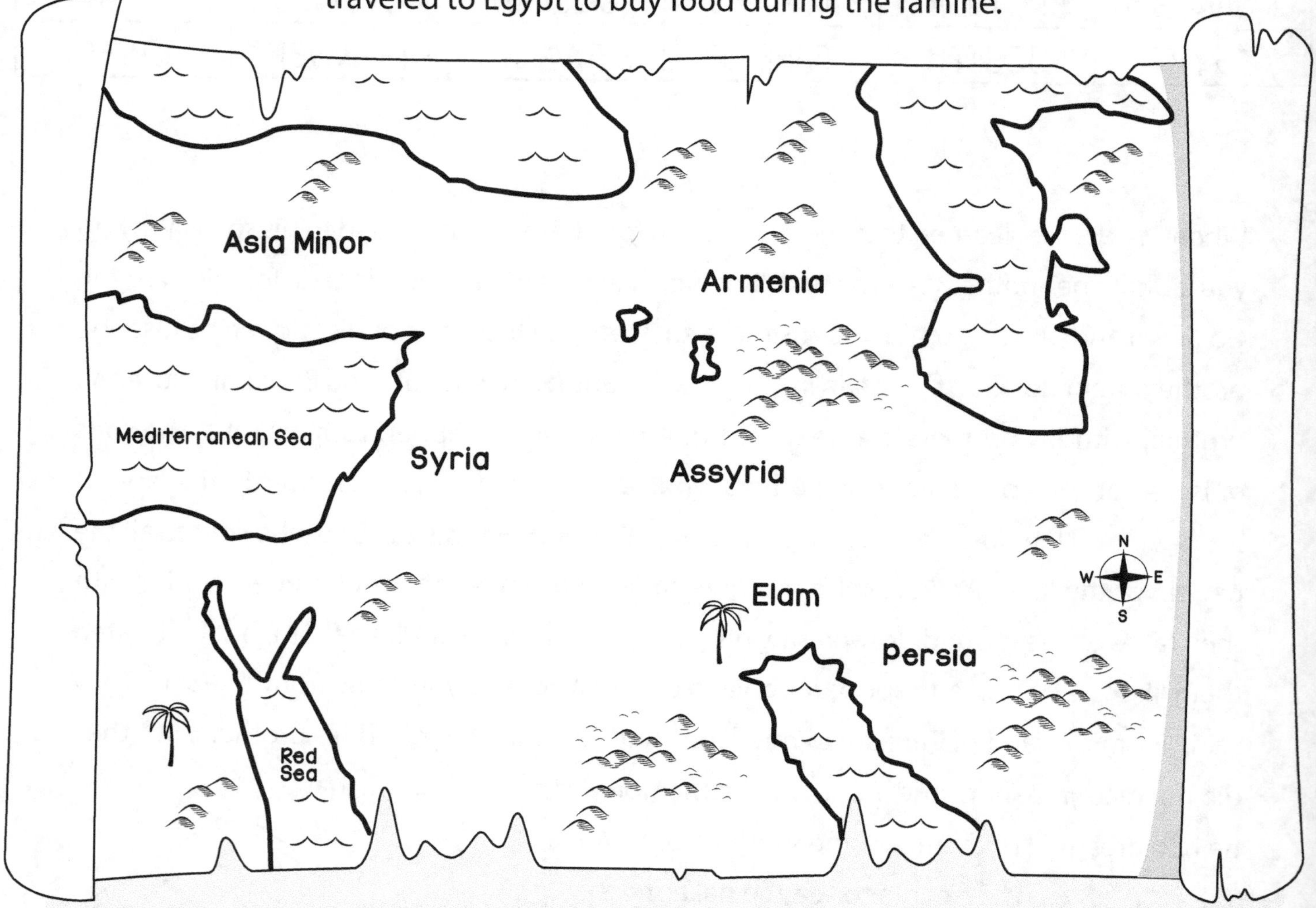

Asia Minor

Armenia

Mediterranean Sea

Syria

Assyria

Elam

Persia

Red Sea

How do you think people traveled to Egypt to buy food during Joseph's time?

....

....

DONKEYS ON THE MOVE

Donkeys were a common sight in Bible times. Israelites from all walks of life owned and rode donkeys, including Abraham, Balaam, the household of King David (Genesis 22:3; Numbers 22:21; Exodus 4:20; 2 Samuel 16:2), and even Yeshua (Mark 11). When Jacob's sons went to Egypt to buy food, they brought grain back to Canaan on donkeys (Genesis 42:26). Later, Joseph sent his father ten donkeys loaded with the best goods of Egypt and ten female donkeys carrying grain, bread, and other supplies for the journey (Genesis 45:23).

Why did the Hebrews love donkeys? Donkeys were known for their strength, intelligence, and loyalty to their owners (Genesis 49:14; Numbers 22:30). They were work animals that carried heavy loads and helped till the soil (Genesis 42:26; Isaiah 30:24). Donkeys also helped guard cattle, sheep, and goats.

Answer the questions below.

1. Who were some of the Israelites in the Bible that owned or rode donkeys?

....

....

2. What did Joseph send to his father using donkeys?

....

....

3. Why do you think donkeys were so important to the Hebrews?

....

....

Spies in Egypt?

Joseph accused his brothers of being spies (Genesis 42:1-34). A spy is someone who secretly collects and reports information about people and activities. What do you think - were Reuben and his brothers really spies? Now, let's create your own pair of binoculars.

You will need:
1. Two paper toilet rolls
2. White or colored paper
3. Scissors (adults-only)
4. Felt pens or crayons
5. School glue, tape, or glue stick
6. Hole punch and string/yarn

Instructions:

1. Paste a piece of white or colored paper around each toilet roll.
2. Ask your child to decorate each toilet roll.
3. Tape the two rolls together using a piece of tape at each end.
4. Create a hole in the outer side of each tube. Thread yarn or string through to create a neck strap.

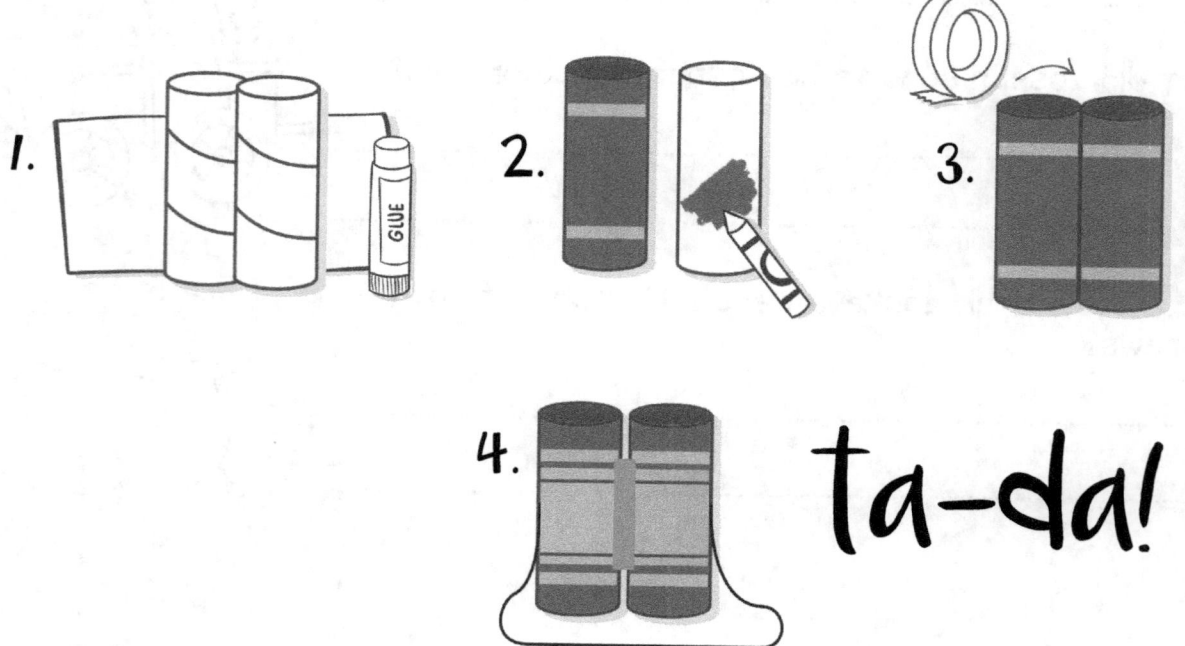

ta-da!

Spies in EGYPT?

Read Genesis 41:46-42:35. Answer the questions below.

1. How old was Joseph when he began serving Pharaoh?

2. What did Joseph do during the seven years of plenty in Egypt?

3. Why did Joseph store grain in every city across Egypt?

4. What were the names of Joseph's two sons, and what did their names mean?

5. What happened after the seven years of plenty in Egypt?

6. What did Pharaoh tell the people of Egypt to do when they asked for bread during the famine?

7. Why did Joseph's brothers go to Egypt?

8. How did Joseph react when he saw his brothers in Egypt, and did they recognize him?

9. What did Joseph accuse his brothers of when they came to buy food?

10. What did Joseph's brothers find in their grain sacks on their way home, and how did they feel about it?

A special meal

> "They served Joseph by himself and them by themselves, and the Egyptians who ate with him by themselves, because the Egyptians could not eat with the Hebrews, for that is an abomination to the Egyptians… Portions were taken to the brothers from Joseph's table, but Benjamin's portion was five times more than any of theirs."
>
> (Genesis 43:31-34)

Joseph invited his brothers to a meal. What food do you think Joseph and his brothers ate? The ancient Egyptians loved to eat garlic, green vegetables, lentils, figs, dates, onions, fish, birds, eggs, cheese, and butter. Bread was often sweetened with dates, honey, or figs and made from barley or wheat. Beer was the most common drink in ancient Egypt. Fish was eaten either roasted or dried and salted. Draw a selection of typical Egyptian food on the table and plates below.

Judah   Simeon   Benjamin

Joseph tests his brothers

Read Genesis 44:1-34. Answer the questions below.

Which man's sack of food contained the silver cup?

After Joseph's official found the silver cup, how did Joseph's brothers respond?

What did Joseph's official say to his brothers?

What animal did Joseph's brothers take with them?

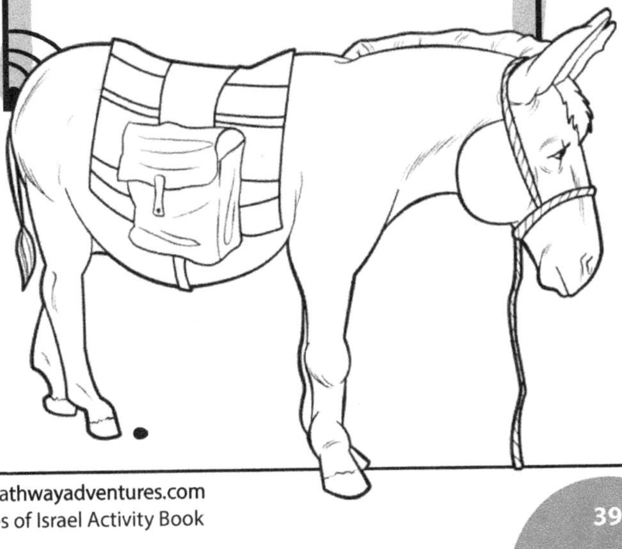

At Joseph's house, which brother spoke to Joseph? What did he say?

Where is Joseph's cup?

**Read Genesis 44:1-13. In the space below, describe what
happened when Joseph's servant found the missing silver cup.
Then, in the speech bubbles above, write the men's conversation.**

....

....

....

....

....

The silver cup

Read Genesis 43:1-44:34 and review the ten sentences below. They recount the story of the silver cup, but they're out of order! Your task is to arrange the sentences correctly. Write a number next to each sentence to sequence the events in their proper order.

A. .... Joseph invited his brothers to a meal at his house, making them nervous because they feared they were in trouble.

B. .... Judah reminded Jacob that they could not return without their youngest brother, Benjamin.

C. .... The famine was severe, and Jacob told his sons to return to Egypt to buy more food.

D. .... Before they left, Joseph tested his brothers by hiding his silver cup in Benjamin's sack.

E. .... Joseph saw how much his brothers had changed and was ready to reveal who he really was.

F. .... During the meal, Joseph gave Benjamin five times as much food as the others.

G. .... When the brothers arrived in Egypt, Joseph saw Benjamin and felt deep compassion for him.

H. .... Jacob reluctantly agreed to send Benjamin to Egypt.

I. .... Judah pleaded with Joseph to take him as a servant instead of Benjamin, as he couldn't bear to return without him.

J. .... The brothers were stopped and accused of stealing the cup, which was found in Benjamin's sack.

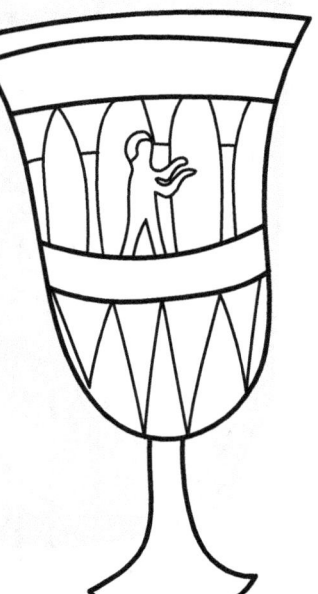

Joseph's secret

Joseph said, "Tell everyone to leave here." So, all the people left. Only the brothers were left with Joseph. Then he told them who he was. Joseph continued to cry, and all the Egyptian people in Pharaoh's house heard it. He said to his brothers, "I am your brother Joseph. Is my father doing well?" But the brothers did not answer him because they were confused and afraid." (Genesis 45:1-3)

1. Read Genesis 45:1-15. Why do you think Joseph's brothers were confused and afraid?

....

....

2. Read Genesis 45:4-8. Why did Yah send Joseph to the land of Egypt?

....

....

EPHRAIM

Read Genesis 48:13.

Joseph's two sons became the tribes of:

The Pharaoh

The Pharaoh was the king of Egypt. He wore a crown with the image of the cobra goddess. Only the Pharaoh could wear this crown. Legend says the goddess protected the Pharaoh by spitting flames at his enemies. While Joseph was alive, the Pharaoh invited Joseph's family to move to the land of Egypt and live in the land of Goshen, where they would have plenty of food and good pasture for their animals.
Draw the right side of the Pharaoh as a mirror image of the left side.

Fun fact:
Pharaohs wore special crowns to show their power and that they were the leader of Egypt.

Did Joseph build a canal?

Did you know there are still signs of Joseph's influence in Egypt? One example is the oasis town of Medinet-el-Faiyum, about eighty miles south of Cairo. This area is full of gardens because of an ancient canal called Bahr Yusuf. In Arabic, "Bahr Yusuf" means "the waterway of Joseph."

In the late 1800s, an American engineer named Francis Cope Whitehouse studied the water source for a small lake called Lake Qarun. He found ruins of ancient dams, ditches, aqueducts, and a canal system that followed the Nile River for many miles. He also found signs that the large basin of el-Faiyum was turned into an artificial lake in ancient times. People believed the stored water helped supply the Nile during dry years. According to local stories, Joseph built the canal and the lake in 1,000 days - 'alf yum' in Arabic. Today, the Bahr Yusuf canal still flows and continues to water the lake.

1. What did Francis Cope Whitehouse discover in the late 19th century?

   ....

   ....

2. Think about life in ancient Egypt. Why do you think Joseph built a canal?

   ....

   ....

Israel moves to EGYPT

Read Genesis 45:1-46:34 (ESV). Complete the crossword below.

ACROSS

4) Israel took all his _____ with him into Egypt.

6) "…take _____ from the land of Egypt for your little ones and your wives…"

8) Joseph's brothers were all _____.

10) All the persons of the house of Jacob who came into Egypt were _____.

DOWN

1) Joseph was ruler of all the land of _____.

2) Joseph sent his father _____ female donkeys.

3) "Israel said, 'It is enough; _____ my son is still alive…'"

5) Joseph gave Benjamin _____ changes of clothes.

7) Joseph and Israel were reunited in this place.

9) Firstborn son of Israel (Jacob).

www.biblepathwayadventures.com
Twelve Tribes of Israel Activity Book

© BPA Publishing Ltd 2022

Jacob blesses his sons

Before he died, Jacob said to his sons, "Gather yourselves together, that I may tell you what shall happen to you in days to come." Read Genesis 49:1-33 and write each son's blessing next to their picture. Then, discuss: Why do you think Jacob gave different blessings to each of his sons?

Reuben:
....
....
....
....

Simeon and Levi:
....
....
....
....

Judah:
....
....
....
....

Zebulun:
....
....
....
....

Issachar:
....
....
....
....

Dan:
....
....
....
....

Jacob blesses his sons

Gad:
....
....
....
....

Asher:
....
....
....
....

Naphtali:
....
....
....
....

Joseph:
....
....
....
....

Benjamin:
....
....
....
....

Decode the
HIEROGLYPHICS!

"There was no food in all the land, for the famine was severe, so that the land of Egypt and the land of Canaan languished by reason of the famine. Joseph gathered up all the money that was found in the land of Egypt and in the land of Canaan, in exchange for the grain that they bought. Joseph brought the money into Pharaoh's house. When the money was all spent in Egypt and in Canaan, all the Egyptians came to Joseph and said, "Give us food. Why should we die before your eyes? For our money is gone."

(Genesis 47:13-15).

a		h		o		v	
b		i		p		w	
c		j		q		x	
d		k		r		y	
e		l		s		z	
f		m		t			
g		n		u			

What did the Egyptians give Joseph in exchange for food? Use the Egyptian alphabet to decode the answers.

....

✳ Read Genesis 47:18-22. How did Pharaoh get all the land in Egypt? How did all the Egyptians become servants?

Moses and the Exodus

Slavery in ancient Egypt

1. Read Exodus 1. Why was Pharaoh worried about the Hebrews?

   ....

   ....

2. What did the Egyptians make the people of Israel do?

   ....

   ....

3. What did Pharaoh tell the Hebrew midwives to do to every Hebrew boy that was born?

   ....

   ....

Goshen

Giza

Memphis

UPPER EGYPT

Nile River

Thebes

N
W E
S

Hebrew slaves in Egypt?

Long ago, during the time of Pharaoh Sobekhotep, many servants in Egypt had Hebrew names. One old Egyptian document, called the Brooklyn Papyrus, listed 95 servants, and about half of them had Hebrew names. Some were called "Asiatic," meaning they came from western Asia, or the land of Canaan, just like Joseph in the Bible. When these servants came to Egypt, they were often given Egyptian names. Many of the servants were women, as they worked in homes, while men usually worked in fields or on construction projects. Around 30 of these servants had names similar to Hebrew.

In other parts of Egypt, wall paintings show scenes that match stories from the Bible. One painting shows slaves from Canaan making bricks with mud and straw, while taskmasters forced them to work, just like in Exodus. Other inscriptions talk about people worshipping "Yahweh," God's name, and shepherds from Canaan living in the Nile Delta, like the Israelites in Genesis. These paintings and writings give us clues about what life was like for the Hebrews in Egypt.

1. Read Exodus 5. Why did Pharaoh tell the Hebrews to make bricks without straw?

   ....

2. Read Genesis 46:33-34. Why do you think the Egyptians did not like the Hebrew shepherds?

   ....

3. Do you think Hebrew names prove that the Hebrews lived in Egypt?

   ....

   ....

Saving baby Moses

Moses' mother saved her son from Pharaoh's cruel order. Read each statement about how this happened, then decide if the statement is true or false by checking the correct box. Use what you know from Exodus 1:1-2:10 to help you answer.

True or False?

Pharaoh treated the Hebrews kindly and gave them plenty of food. ⬭ **True** ⬭ **False**

Moses' mother hid him for three months to protect him from Pharaoh. ⬭ **True** ⬭ **False**

Pharaoh wanted to keep all the baby boys safe in Egypt. ⬭ **True** ⬭ **False**

Moses' sister, Miriam, watched to see what would happen to him after he was placed in the basket. ⬭ **True** ⬭ **False**

Pharaoh's daughter found Moses in a basket among the reeds. ⬭ **True** ⬭ **False**

Moses was found by a Hebrew woman who adopted him as her son. ⬭ **True** ⬭ **False**

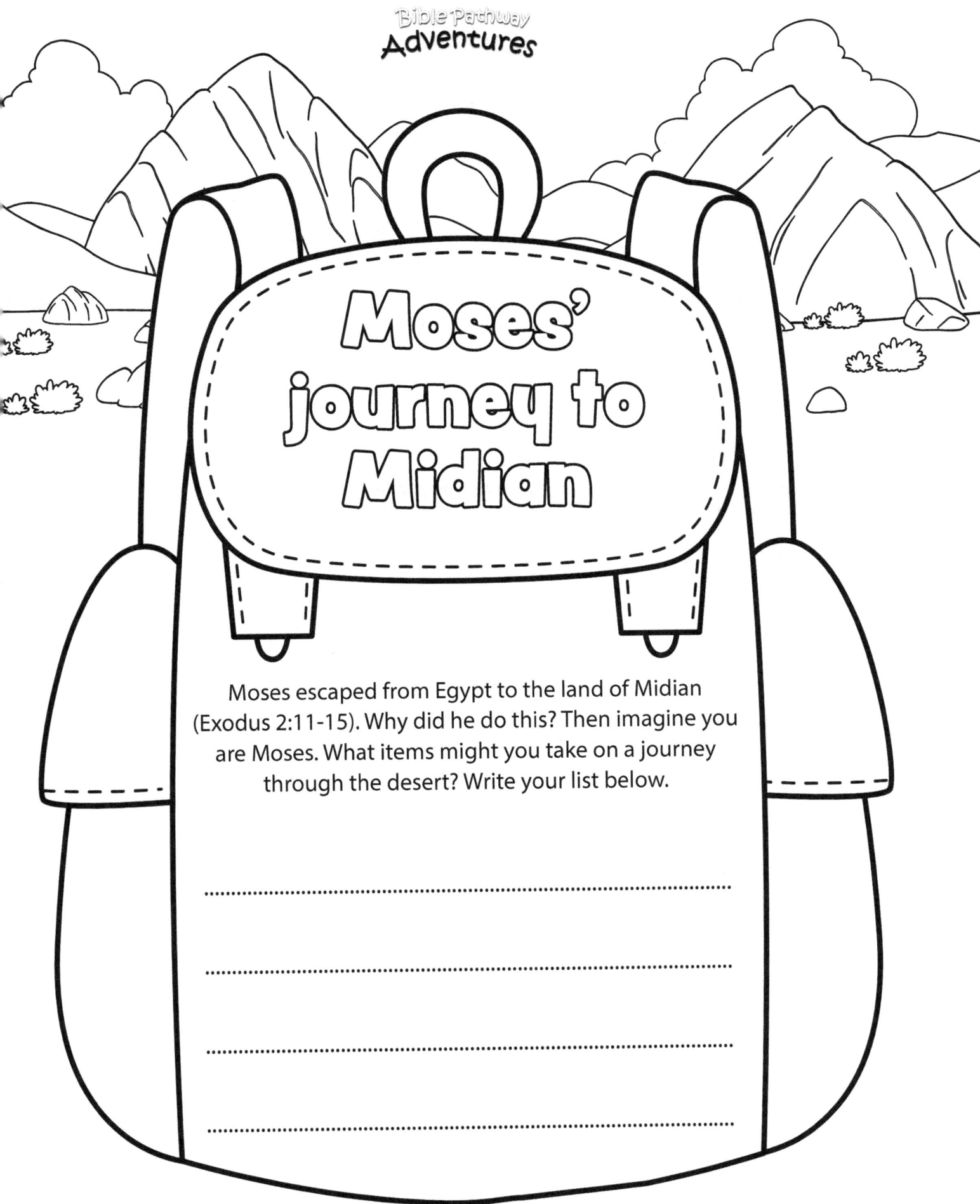

Moses' journey to Midian

Moses escaped from Egypt to the land of Midian (Exodus 2:11-15). Why did he do this? Then imagine you are Moses. What items might you take on a journey through the desert? Write your list below.

....

....

....

....

Moses in MIDIAN

Read Exodus 2:11-3:1. Answer the questions below.

1. Why did Moses kill the Egyptian?

2. How did Pharaoh react when he heard that Moses had killed the Egyptian?

3. To which land did Moses escape?

4. Where did Moses meet Jethro's daughters?

5. Who drove the shepherds away from the well?

6. How did Jethro (Reuel) react when he heard that Moses had helped his daughters?

7. Who did Moses marry?

8. Who was Moses' first son?

9. What was Jethro's job?

10. What did Moses do while he lived in the wilderness?

Signs at Mount Horeb

Read Exodus 4:1-17. Yah gave Moses special signs near Mount Horeb to show His power. These signs helped Moses prove Yah was with him. Read the questions below and write your answers.

Moses' staff turns into a snake. What does this sign show you about Yah's power?

....
....
....
....
....
....
....
....
....
....

Moses' hand turns leprous then heals. Why do you think Yah used this sign?

....
....
....
....
....
....
....
....
....
....

Moses and Aaron spoke to Pharaoh, and asked him to free the children of Israel (Exodus 7:1-14). Unscramble the words to learn the people and objects mentioned in this Bible passage.

PHARAOH!

ahPharo ....

essMo ....

ronAa ....

tsfaf ....

astnresv ....

ethar ....

aenrhedd ....

rsentpe ....

Let My people go!

Moses and Aaron went to Pharaoh and asked him to let the children of Israel go (Exodus 5:1-2). How did Pharaoh respond? Write their conversation in the speech bubbles above. Then, write below how Pharaoh made life harder for the Hebrews.

....

....

....

....

Ten plagues challenge

Read Exodus 7:14–11:10. Put the plagues in the correct order.
Write a number in the square to show the order in which each one happened.

Water to blood

livestock die

flies

lice

fiery hail

darkness

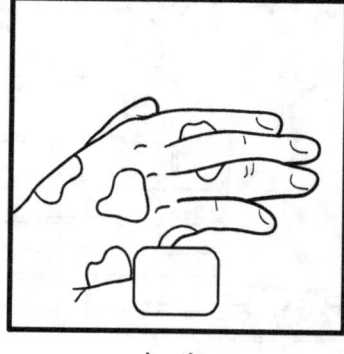
boils

frogs

locusts

death of firstborn

Ten plagues, ten false gods

The Egyptians worshipped many false gods, but the ten plagues showed they weren't as powerful as Yahweh, the God of Abraham, Isaac, and Jacob. The '**Ten plagues of Egypt**' column shows what Yahweh did to show His power. The '**Egyptian false gods**' column lists their gods—but in a mixed-up order! Read about the Egyptian gods below, then draw a line from each plague to the Egyptian god it challenged. Can you match them all?

Ten plagues of Egypt

Turned the Nile River into blood

Sent frogs all over Egypt

Sent lice to cover people and animals

Sent swarms of flies everywhere

Made the Egyptian livestock die

Sent boils on people and animals

Sent fiery hail from the sky

Sent locusts to eat all the crops

Made darkness cover Egypt
for three days

Struck down the firstborn
in Egypt

Egyptian false gods

Osiris

Geb

Ra

Hathor

Hapi

Khepri

Pharaoh

Isis

Nut

Heqet

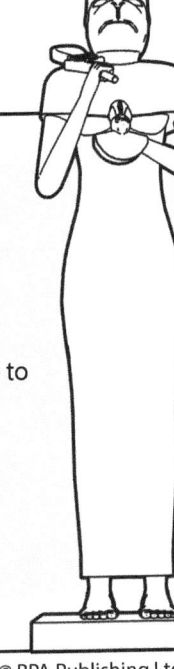

False Egyptian gods

- **Hapi:** God of the Nile River
- **Heqet:** Frog-headed goddess of birth
- **Geb:** God of the earth
- **Khepri:** Scarab beetle god linked to insects
- **Hathor:** Cow goddess of protection
- **Isis:** Goddess of magic and healing

- **Nut:** The sky goddess
- **Osiris:** God of crops and the underworld
- **Ra:** The sun god
- **Pharaoh:** The Egyptians' divine ruler, unable to save the firstborn

The first Passover

When Pharaoh refused to free the people of Israel, God decided to strike every firstborn in the land of Egypt. But first, He told Moses how His people could protect themselves from the final plague.
Read Exodus 12:1-32. Answer the questions.

1. What did Moses tell the elders of Israel to do to avoid the final plague?

2. How long were the Israelites told to honor the Pesach?

3. What did the Israelites eat for the first Passover meal?

4. Describe the tenth plague.

5. What type of bread were the Israelites told to eat for seven days?

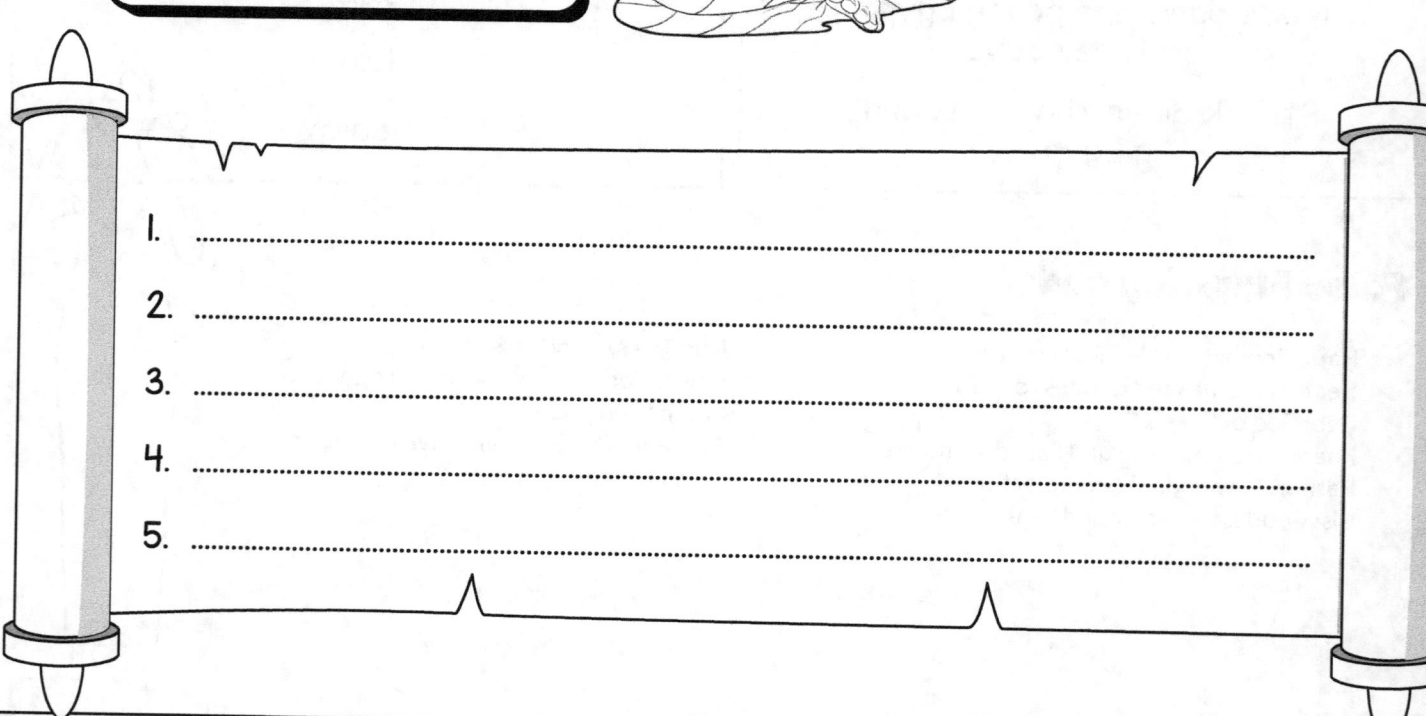

1. ....
2. ....
3. ....
4. ....
5. ....

Imagine you are a Hebrew living in the land of Egypt. Write a report about what happened the night you observed the first Passover.

Matzah

The Hebrew name for unleavened bread is Matzah. Matzah is a type of bread made from flour and water. Matzah is eaten during one of God's Appointed Times, the Feast of Unleavened Bread, to remind the Israelites of the time when they had to leave Egypt in such a hurry that their bread didn't have time to rise. To make matzah, you mix flour and water, roll it out very thin, and bake it quickly. Since it doesn't contain yeast, it stays flat and crispy. How do you make matzah during the Feast of Unleavened Bread?

Matzah
(Mah-TSAH)
מַצָּה
Unleavened bread

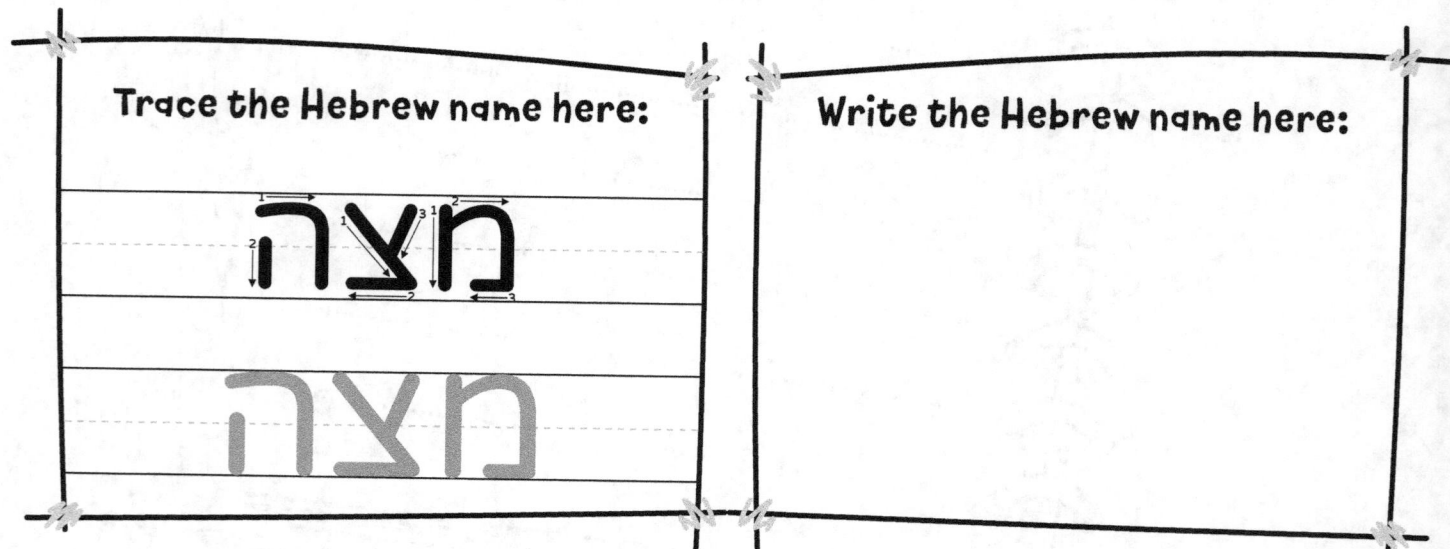

Trace the Hebrew name here:

מצה

מצה

Write the Hebrew name here:

Let's write!

Practice writing the Hebrew name for unleavened bread on the lines below.

מצה

Try this on your own.
Remember that Hebrew is read from RIGHT to LEFT.

Why do you think it's important for Israelites to eat matzah during the Feast of Unleavened Bread?

....

....

....

....

Feast of Unleavened BREAD

Read Exodus 12:1-51. Find and circle the words below.

```
A U D W W Z Y R F V Y M A D D
R P N X J E O A I L R A A W C
W X P L L I P P H B P T I E O
A O O O E D K U F W W Z S L N
X O B I I A Y Z E B E A E L G
E V S H S N V T W U T H V I R
J D E R Z R T E X Z L Q E N E
X K R S A D D E N Q O H N G G
W I V Z P H U X D E K U D P A
Q Q E K H K E F S T D F A L T
E G Y P T K X E U P I S Y A I
F O R E V E R A Z H P M S C O
C M D L P H B S G V Y H E E N
V H N N O K T T V G M L D A R
D Y V I S R A E L I T E S Z C
```

DWELLING PLACE

FEAST

EGYPT

FOREVER

CONGREGATION

MATZAH

OBSERVE

YAHWEH

ISRAELITES

UNLEAVENED

SEVEN DAYS

APPOINTED TIME

Feast of Unleavened Bread

The Feast of Unleavened Bread is one of Yah's Appointed Times (Leviticus 23) and has been celebrated for thousands of years. It began when Yah freed the Israelites from slavery in Egypt, as told in Exodus 12. He told them to leave quickly, so they made bread without yeast, called unleavened bread, because there was not enough time to let it rise. In their hurry, the Israelites also took their dough that had not risen yet, along with their kneading bowls. This Feast lasts for seven days and begins with the Passover meal.

Centuries later, Israelites from many places traveled to Jerusalem to worship at the Temple during this Feast. Before the Feast of Unleavened Bread, Yeshua came to Jerusalem and rode in on a donkey. The Israelites cheered and hoped He would be their king and save them from the Romans. But Yah had a different plan. While the Israelites were eating their Passover meal, remembering the lamb's blood that saved them in Egypt, Yeshua was crucified outside the city. He became the ultimate Passover Lamb, taking away the sins of the world, as it says in John 1:29: "Behold, the Lamb of God, who takes away the sin of the world."

1. What is unleavened bread, and why did the Israelites make it when they left Egypt?

....

....

2. Why do you think Yah wanted the Israelites to leave Egypt so quickly?

....

....

3. Why do you think Yah told the Israelites to eat bread without yeast during this Feast?

....

....

"God guided them with a pillar of cloud by day and a pillar of fire by night..."

(Exodus 13:21)

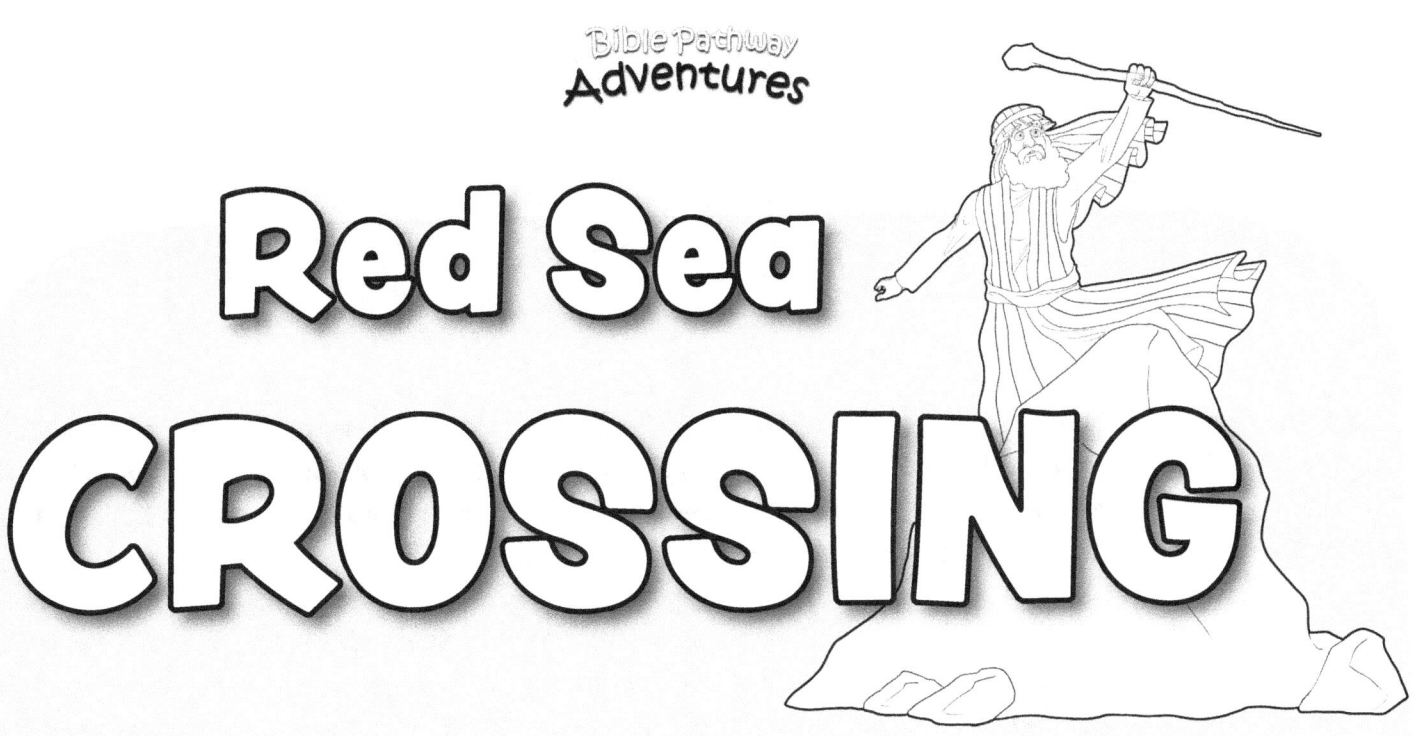

Red Sea CROSSING

Read Exodus 13:17-15:1. Answer the questions below.

1. Who led the Israelites out of Egypt?

2. Whose bones did the Israelites take with them?

3. Who guided the Israelites through the wilderness?

4. Which army chased after the Israelites?

5. When the Israelites reached the sea, where did they camp?

6. How did Moses command the sea to divide so the Israelites could cross to the other side?

7. Which sea did the Israelites cross through to escape the Egyptians?

8. How did God stop the Egyptians from chasing the Israelites across the sea?

9. What happened to the Egyptian army?

10. What did the Israelites do when they reached the other side of the sea?

Red Sea discovery?

At the time of the Exodus, Egypt controlled the Sinai Peninsula. To escape the Egyptian army quickly, the Israelites had to cross the Red Sea to leave Egypt. Bible scholars are not sure where the Red Sea crossing took place. Some think it might have been at Lake Sirbonis in Egypt, while others believe it happened at the Port of Suez or the Straits of Tiran.

A group of archaeologists believes the Israelites crossed the Red Sea at Nuweiba Beach, located on the Gulf of Aqaba, facing Saudi Arabia. This beach is so big that you can see it on satellite maps! Divers and scientists found an underwater land bridge between Nuweiba Beach and the Saudi Arabian coastline. Even more amazing, archaeologists discovered coral-covered chariot wheels and fossilized animal bones on the sea floor! Some wheels were still attached to axles, while others were not. They also found chariot cabs without wheels, just like the Bible says when God made the Egyptians' chariot wheels fall off (Exodus 14:24-25). Human and horse skeletons, including skulls, hipbones, and hooves, were also found partly covered by coral.

What do you think? Could Nuweiba Beach be the actual site of the crossing? Why / why not?

....

....

....

....

Song of Moses

(Exodus 15:1-4)

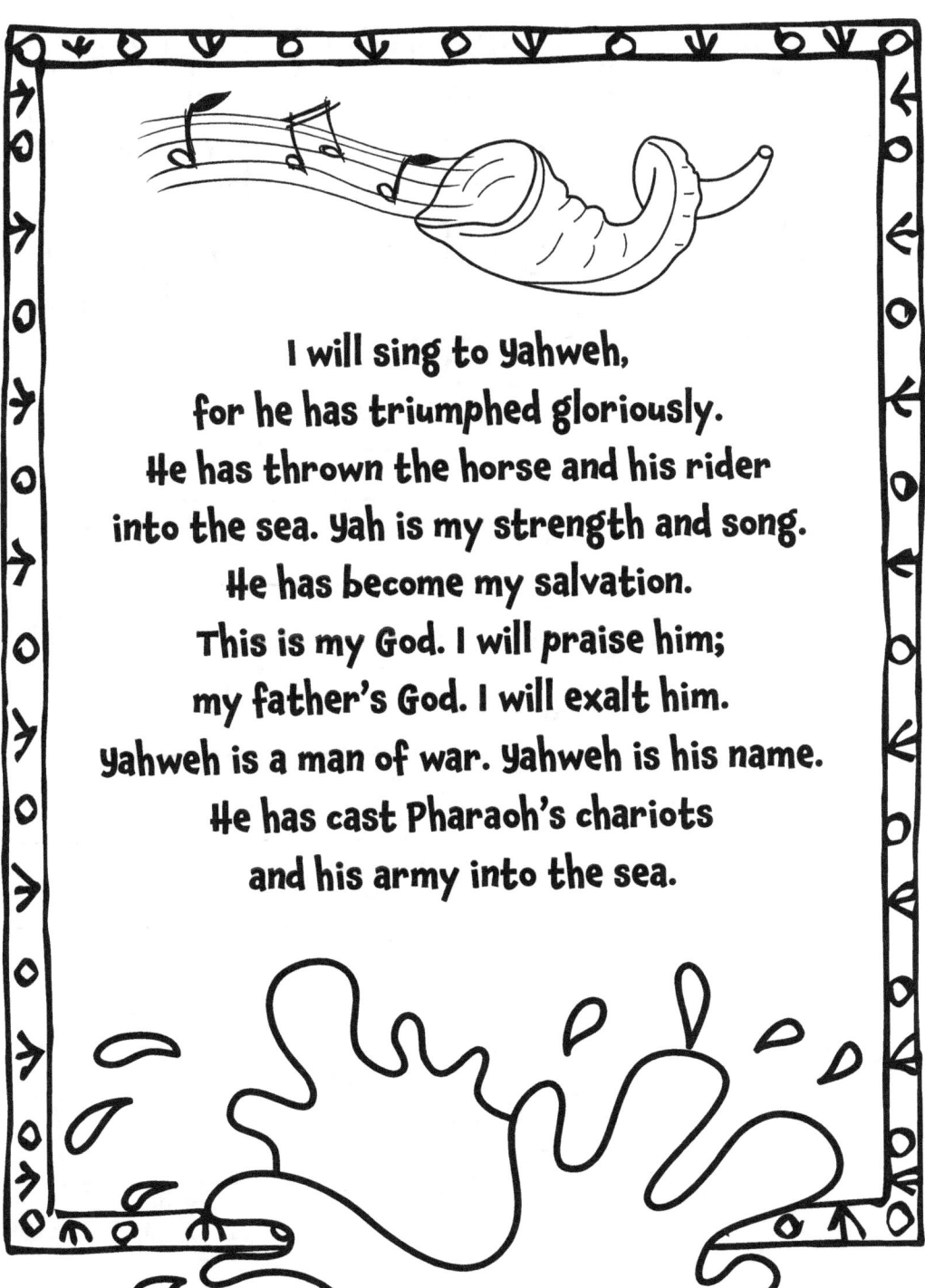

I will sing to Yahweh,
for he has triumphed gloriously.
He has thrown the horse and his rider
into the sea. Yah is my strength and song.
He has become my salvation.
This is my God. I will praise him;
my father's God. I will exalt him.
Yahweh is a man of war. Yahweh is his name.
He has cast Pharaoh's chariots
and his army into the sea.

God provides!

Read Exodus 16:1-36. The Israelites were hungry in the wilderness.
What did God give them to eat? Each number below represents a letter of the alphabet
(A = 1, B = 2, etc.). Replace each number with its letter to reveal the answer.

A 1	B 2	C 3	D 4	E 5	F 6	G 7	H 8	I 9	J 10	K 11	L 12	M 13
N 14	O 15	P 16	Q 17	R 18	S 19	T 20	U 21	V 22	W 23	X 24	Y 25	Z 26

1   7 – 15 – 4: _____

2   7 – 1 – 22 – 5: _____

3   20 – 8 – 5: _____

4   9 – 19 – 18 – 1 – 5 – 12 – 9 – 20 – 5 – 19: _____

5   13 – 1 – 14 – 14 – 1: _____

6   1 – 14 – 4: _____

7   17 – 21 – 1 – 9 – 12: _____

8   20 – 15: _____

9   5 – 1 – 20: _____

Miracles at Rephidim

Read Exodus 17:1-16 and review the ten sentences below. They recount the story of the Israelites at Rephidim, but they're out of order! Your task is to arrange the sentences in the correct sequence. Write a number next to each sentence to show the proper order of events.

A. .... Moses named the place Massah and Meribah because the people tested God, asking, "Is God among us or not?"

B. .... With Moses' hands raised, Joshua's men defeated Amalek, and Moses built an altar, calling it "Yahweh Is My Banner" to remember God's help.

C. .... The Amalekites attacked Israel at Rephidim.

D. .... When Moses held up his hands, Israel won; when he lowered them, Amalek gained, so Aaron and Hur held his hands steady.

E. .... The people argued with Moses, demanding water and questioning why he brought them out of the land of Egypt.

F. .... At Horeb, God told Moses to strike a rock, and water flowed out for the people to drink.

G. .... Moses told Joshua to gather men to fight, while he went to a hilltop with God's staff.

H. .... God told Moses to go ahead with some of the elders of Israel and take the staff he used at the Nile River.

I. .... The Israelites moved from the wilderness and camped at Rephidim, where there was no water.

J. .... Moses asked God for help, fearing the people might stone him.

Jethro's wise advice

Read Exodus 18:13–27. When Moses tried to judge all the Israelite's problems by himself, it made him very tired! His father-in-law, Jethro, gave him wise advice to choose helpers and share the work. Below is an organization chart showing how Moses followed Jethro's advice. Fill in the chart using the information from Exodus 18. Then, answer the questions below.

Moses

Answer the questions.

1. Why was it a good idea for Moses to choose leaders to help him?

....

....

2. What kind of Israelites did Moses choose to be leaders?

....

....

Mount Sinai and the Covenant

The shofar blast

"On the morning of the third day, there were thunders and lightnings, a thick cloud on the mountain, and a very loud trumpet (shofar) blast, so that all the people in the camp trembled." (Exodus 19:16) The Hebrew word for "trumpet" in this verse is *shofar*. A *shofar* is made from a ram's horn and was used to signal important events. In the Bible, the *shofar* was often blown to gather people, announce certain Appointed Times (Feasts), proclaim the coronation of kings, and signal war.

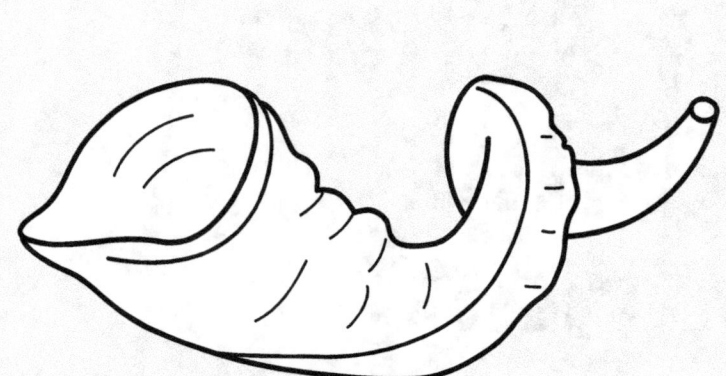

Shofar
(Shoh-FAHR)

שׁוֹפָר

Trumpet

Trace the Hebrew word here:

שׁוֹפָר

שׁוֹפָר

Write the Hebrew word here:

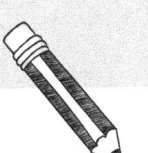

Let's write!

Practice writing this Hebrew word on the lines below.

שׁופֿר

שופר

Try this on your own.
Remember that Hebrew is read from RIGHT to LEFT.

Read Exodus 19:16-20. How do you think the Israelites felt when they heard the loud shofar blast at Mount Sinai?

....
....
....
....

"There were thunders and lightnings and a thick cloud on the mountain and a very loud shofar blast..."

(Exodus 19:16)

The ten commandments

Read Exodus 20.
Write the ten commandments
on the tablets.

The ten
COMMANDMENTS

Read Exodus 20:1-17. Find and circle the words below.

```
D N X F Q U P B I K W Q W G D
O O H Z E K R E S C N Q S F O
N O S N Y G J Q A O E X L A N
O T J Z V K T P E L I Q J L O
T H H J H I A J L R G M P S T
C E A O C S Q S I B H D O E M
O R T S A B B A T H B H V W U
V G H L S F Y D E G O H D I R
E O L O B N V B S E R Y S T D
T D S R N I J W V G Y M R N E
C S D O N O T S T E A L J E R
S V B Z R F R F I X D H J S R
P T A B L E T S H C K D V S Q
C O M M A N D M E N T S Z X X
D U M C E G F U N H O L Y B O
```

TABLETS

HOLY

DO NOT COVET

DO NOT MURDER

COMMANDMENTS

FALSE WITNESS

HONOR

SABBATH

ISRAELITES

NO OTHER GODS

DO NOT STEAL

NEIGHBOR

Camp of Israel

In the wilderness, Yah told the Israelites to camp in a certain way.
They camped in tribes on each side of the camp. Yah chose the tribe of Levi
to serve as priests. They camped around the tabernacle. Read Numbers 2.
In a banner above each tent, write the name of a tribe of Israel.

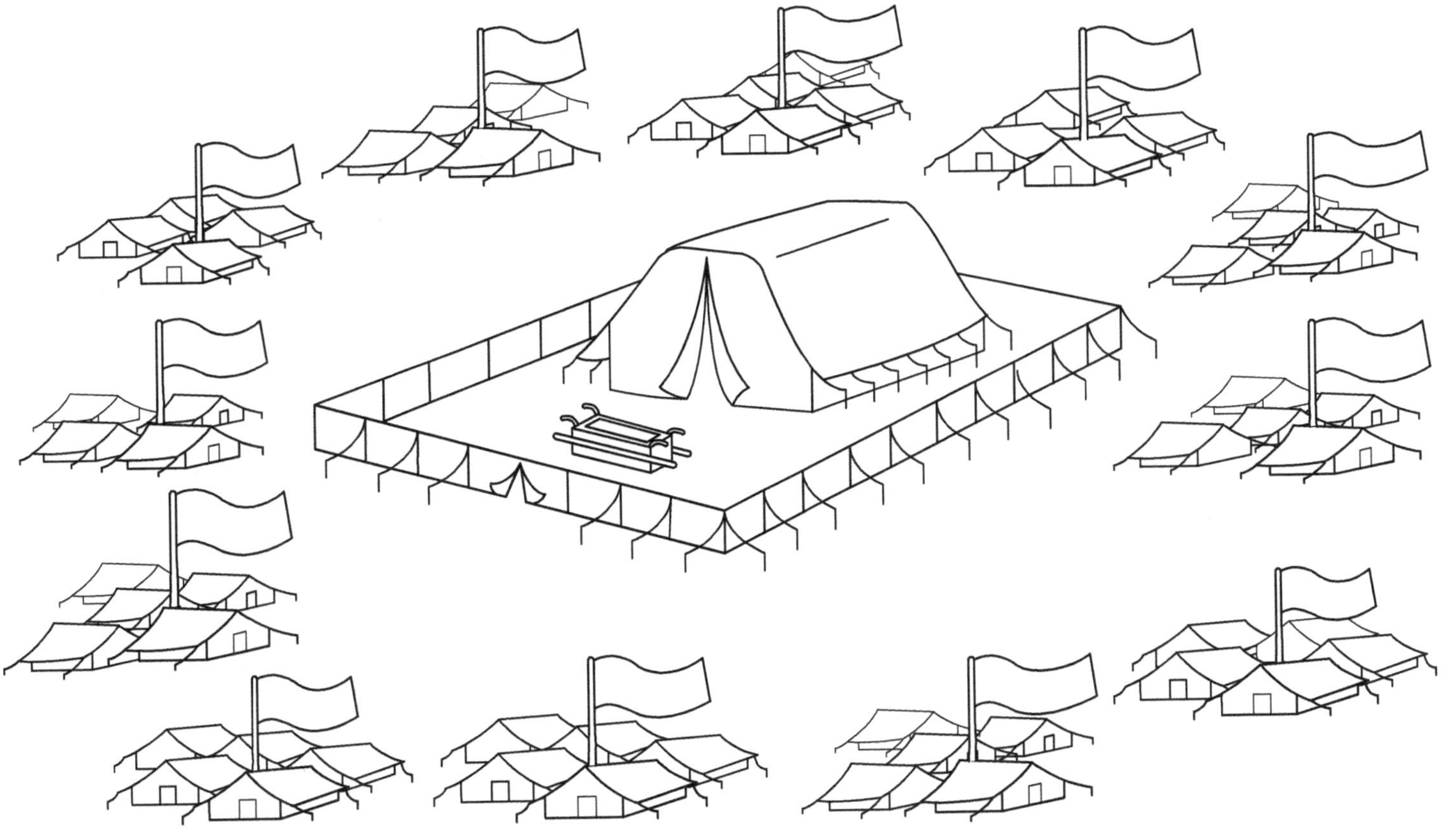

Twelve tribes of Israel

After the Israelites left Egypt, they spent 40 years in the wilderness learning how to follow Yah's instructions before they reached the land of Canaan. The Israelites were split into twelve tribes, although in fact there were thirteen tribes. Each tribe was named after a son or grandson of Israel (Jacob); eleven of Jacob's sons headed one tribe each, while the descendants of Joseph became two separate tribes (Ephraim and Manasseh). Why do you think God divided the Israelites into tribes? Where are the tribes today? Color the banners from the twelve tribes of Israel mentioned in Numbers 1:1-15 and 13:4-15.

ISSACHAR

JUDAH

ZEBULUN

NAPHTALI

ASHER

DAN

Twelve tribes of Israel

GAD

SIMEON

REUBEN

EPHRAIM

MANASSEH

BENJAMIN

Twelve tribes of Israel

The <u>descendants</u> of the 12 sons of Jacob (Israel) became the 12 tribes of Israel.

Sons

Reuben
Simeon
Levi
Judah
Dan
Naphtali
Gad
Asher
Issachar
Zebulun
Joseph
Benjamin

Tribes

Reuben
Simeon
~~Levi~~
Judah
Dan
Naphtali
Gad
Asher
Issachar
Zebulun
~~Joseph~~ Manasseh & Ephraim
Benjamin

Levi got no land but had to look after the tabernacle

Joseph was divided into two tribes: Manasseh & Ephraim

** <u>Descendants</u> are people born after the person in the same family.

Unscramble the 12 tribes

Read Numbers 2. Unscramble the tribes to learn the names of the twelve tribes of Israel camped around the tabernacle.

aGd

nubeRe

oniSem

jnBneiam

scrIaahs

mEihrap

uJhda

anD

altNhpai

ersAh

ulnbueZ

aehsMnsa

REUBEN

BENJAMIN

SIMEON

ASHER

Twelve tribes of Israel

The Hebrew people left the land of Egypt and followed Moses through the wilderness for forty years until they reached the land of Canaan. These people became the twelve tribes of Israel. Each tribe was made up of hundreds of thousands of people and was named after a son or grandson of Jacob (whose name was later changed to Israel). Because of this, the Hebrew people became known as the Israelites, or the twelve tribes of Israel. The Bible describes Israel as a people.

"Yahweh says: 'Behold, I will take the children of Israel from among the nations, where they have gone, and will gather them on every side and bring them into their own land.'" (Ezekiel 37:21) The names of the tribes were Asher, Dan, Ephraim, Gad, Issachar, Manasseh, Naphtali, Reuben, Simeon, Levi, Joseph, and Zebulun. Each tribe had its own standard and symbol.

1. Why did the Hebrews become known as the tribes of Israel?

    ....

    ....

2. Where do you think the tribes of Israel live today?

    ....

    ....

3. Why do you think each tribe had its own symbol?

    ....

    ....

The Tabernacle and the wilderness

The golden CALF

Read Exodus 32:1-35. Complete the crossword below.

ACROSS

2) The people made a golden _____ to worship.

4) Aaron shaped the golden calf using a _____.

5) The Israelites said, "These are your gods O Israel, who brought you out of _____."

7) Moses told the sons of Levi to take their _____ and go throughout the camp.

8) Moses was on Mount _____ when the people made a gold calf.

9) God wrote His commandments on _____ tablets.

DOWN

1) Moses smashed the _____ when he saw the idol.

3) Aaron told the people to bring their _____ earrings.

6) The Israelites offered burnt offerings and brought _____ offerings.

9) Moses asked God to forgive the Israelites' _____.

Waiting for Moses

When the people saw that Moses delayed in coming down from the mountain, they gathered around Aaron and said, "Make us gods who will go before us. As for Moses, we don't know what has happened to him." What did Aaron do next? Read Exodus 32:1-35 and write Aaron's actions below in your own words.

Answer the questions below.

What was engraved on the tablets?

Who let the Israelites break loose, causing them to be mocked by their enemies?

What was God's promise to Abraham?

Where is Mount Sinai?

Many people believe Mount Sinai is on the Sinai Peninsula in Egypt. But there is no evidence from the Bible or archaeology that shows this is the true location of the biblical Mount Sinai. Let's take a closer look and see what you think. Read the article, then answer the questions on the next page.

Mount Sinai

Did you know the Bible says that Mount Sinai is located in Arabia, not Egypt (Galatians 4:25)? Recently, archaeologists discovered a place that points to Jebel el Lawz in Saudi Arabia as the possible location of the biblical Mount Sinai. This mountain is in northwest Saudi Arabia, near the coast of the Gulf of Aqaba. An aerial map shows that the mountain has an almost semi-circular shape, enclosing an area of 5,000 acres. Unlike nearby mountains, the entire top of Jebel el Lawz is blackened (Exodus 19:18). On the face of Jebel el Lawz, there is evidence of an ancient stream. The Bible says that when Moses destroyed the golden calf, he "cast the dust into the brook that descended out of the mount…" (Deuteronomy 9:21).

In 1985, archaeologists found many large stone columns (or wells) nearby that formed a line along an ancient "lake" area bordering the holy site. Could these wells and lake have been part of a water supply system for the Israelites? The Bible says, "Moses…built an altar under the hill, and twelve pillars according to the twelve tribes of Israel" (Exodus 24:4).

At the base of Jebel el Lawz, archaeologists found an altar similar to the altar of "uncut" stone mentioned in Exodus (Exodus 20:25; 24:4). Next to the altar was an L-shaped structure with walls about three feet thick. Was this area where animals were killed before being sacrificed as a burnt offering? Nearby, archaeologists found twelve large granite boulders about six feet wide and nine feet tall. About two kilometers away from the holy site, they discovered a large stone altar with carvings of Egyptian animal fertility gods. If the Israelites made these carvings, it makes sense they would depict Egyptian gods since they once lived in Egypt.

Where is Mount Sinai?

Look at an atlas and describe where Saudi Arabia is located.

....

....

....

....

....

....

What do you think? Could Jebel el Lawz be the biblical Mount Sinai?

....

....

....

Read the passage on the previous page and do your own research. What evidence have archaeologists found that suggests Jebel el Lawz might be the biblical Mount Sinai?

....

....

....

....

....

....

....

....

....

Discovering the Paleo-Hebrew alphabet

Most modern language scholars trace the English alphabet back to the Phoenician alphabet from the 10th century B.C. This alphabet was made up of pictures and is very similar to the Paleo-Hebrew script, which was used about 1,000 years earlier. The ancient Israelites used the Paleo-Hebrew script to write down their customs and scriptures. Some people wonder if this might be the script Elohim used to engrave the stone tablets on Mount Sinai. Did you know that Paleo-Hebrew inscriptions have been found near Jebel el-Lawz in Saudi Arabia? Some archaeologists believe this could be the real site of the biblical Mount Sinai. What do you think?

Aleph	Bet	Gimmel	Dalet	Hey
Vav	Zayin	Het	Tet	Yod
Kaph	Lamed	Mem	Nun	Samech
Ayin	Peh	Tsadi	Qoph	Resh
Shin	Tav			

Trace each letter, then practice writing it on your own!

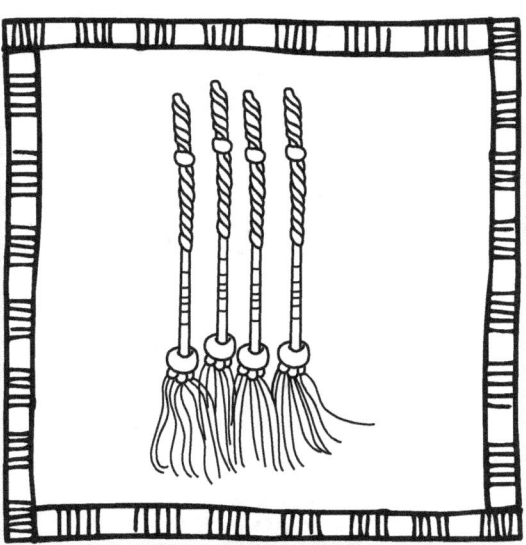

Yah told Moses, "...tell the people of Israel to make tassels on the corners of their garments throughout their generations...".

Read Numbers 15 and Deuteronomy 22. Why did the Israelites start wearing tzitzit (tassels)? What do tzitzit represent?

....

....

....

....

....

....

Bible Pathway Adventures

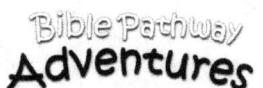

"Remember the Sabbath day, to keep it holy."

(Exodus 20:8)

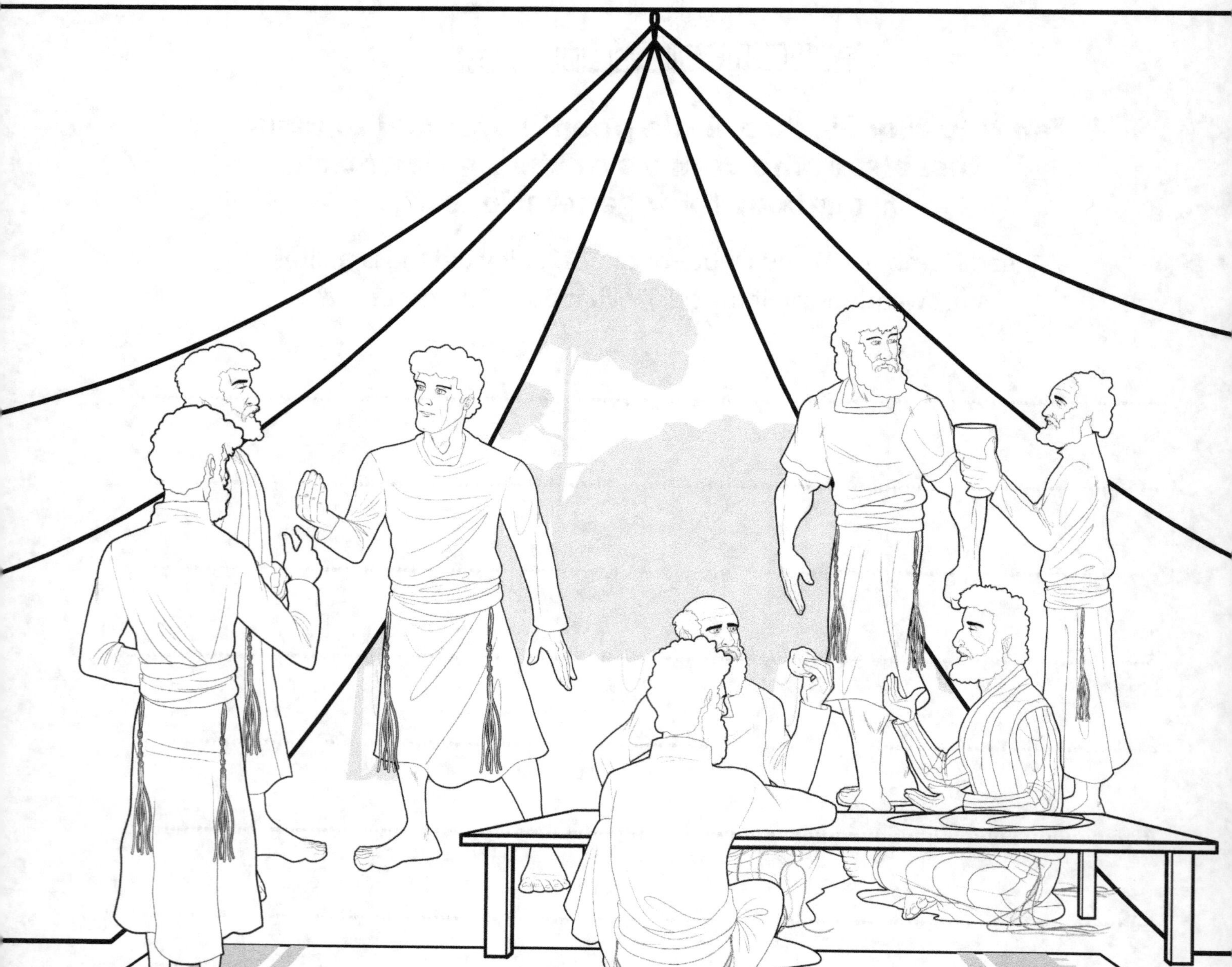

The SABBATH

Read Genesis 2, Exodus 31, Deuteronomy 5, Leviticus 23 - 24, Isaiah 58, Psalm118, Jeremiah 17, and 2 Chronicles 2. Find and circle the words below.

```
P Y B L E S S E D U H A C X W
P D E T R F U P S N F S O W I
S V E K T B J Q A S X C M T T
N E T L V R Y M B E Q B M R O
B O T L I Q D Q B V W T A G R
T W E A D G I N A E J V N X A
H Q K K P F H V T N M W D S H
K O B I H A C T H T D Z M J R
T Q L Y U X R E S H Q T E Z E
K O X Y M M P T Q D N J N E J
Q I H L W N V I B A B B T Q O
Z V F K Q C K W K Y T J K G I
A P P O I N T E D T I M E T C
E V E R L A S T I N G R X R E
V B M Q E Y E S H U A Y C P R
```

DELIGHT

HOLY

SET APART

BLESSED

EVERLASTING

TORAH

REJOICE

SEVENTH DAY

COMMANDMENT

SABBATH

YESHUA

APPOINTED TIME

WHAT ARE HIGH SABBATHS?

Are there days on Yah's calendar other than the weekly Sabbath that are observed as Sabbaths? Yes! Yah set aside special days called Appointed Times for the people of Israel to observe forever (Leviticus 23). These include days known as High Sabbaths, which are different from the regular weekly Sabbath.

THE SPRING FEASTS

The Feast of Unleavened Bread (Chag Ha-Matzot) starts with the Passover meal and lasts for seven days. The first and seventh days of this Feast are High Sabbaths. On these days, no regular work is allowed. The Feast of Pentecost (Shavu'ot) takes place 50 days after the day of First Fruits. It was a time to give thanks for the grain harvest and is also a High Sabbath.

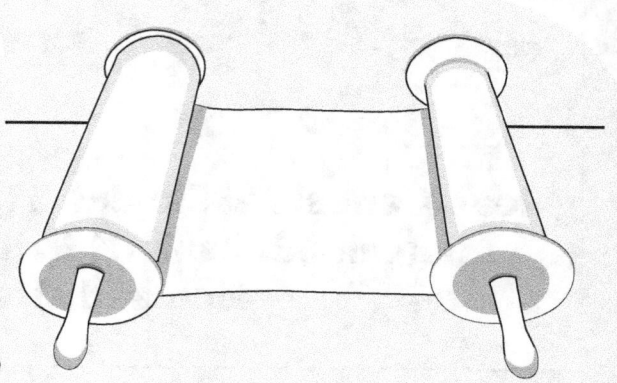

THE FALL FEASTS

The Feast of Trumpets (Yom Teru'ah) occurs on the first day of the seventh month. It is a High Sabbath, even though it does not fall on the seventh day of the week. The Day of Atonement (Yom Kippur) is observed on the tenth day of the seventh month. It is a High Sabbath and a day of complete rest. The Feast of Tabernacles (Sukkot) lasts for seven days. The first day is a High Sabbath, and the eighth day, known as The Last Great Day (Shemini Atzeret), is also a High Sabbath.

How does honoring Yah's Appointed Times help people remember His instructions and promises?

....

....

....

....

Match the Feasts!

Read Leviticus 23 and the list of weekly and annual Appointed Times below.
Then draw a line to match each Appointed Time with its action.

Yah's Appointed Times

The Sabbath Day

The Passover meal and
Unleavened Bread (Nisan 14-20)

Pentecost (Sivan 6-7)

Trumpets (Tishri 1)

Atonement (Tishri 10)

Tabernacles (Tishri 15-21)

Shemini Atzeret (Tishri 22)

Action

Israelites give thanks for the harvest 50 days after the wave offering.

Yah appoints this weekly time for rest and worship.

Represents the 1000-year reign (the Millennial Reign) on earth.

Yah delivers the Israelites from Egypt, and they eat matzah for seven days. This Feast includes two High Sabbaths: one on Day 1 and another on Day 7.

Israelites blow the shofar to mark repentance, preparation, and Yah's kingship.

Israelites fast (affliction) and repent.

A wedding celebration! Israelites live in temporary shelters to remember the Israelites' journey in the wilderness.

Appointed Times
OF THE BIBLE

Read Exodus 13 and 23, Leviticus 23, Deuteronomy 5, 1 Kings 8, Acts 2 and 27. Answer the questions below.

1. What does the Bible say to do on the Sabbath?

2. What type of bread do Israelites eat during the Feast of Unleavened Bread?

3. The Passover meal takes place at the start of which Feast?

4. What did the Israelites eat during the first Passover?

5. What were the apostles filled with on Shavuot (Pentecost)?

6. Which three Appointed Times are Biblical pilgrimage festivals?

7. Which Appointed Time did Paul mention in Acts 27:9?

8. On which Appointed Time do you blow a shofar?

9. During which Appointed Time did Solomon dedicate the temple?

10. During which Appointed Time were the Israelites instructed to dwell in temporary shelters?

When does Sukkot begin?

Read Leviticus 23:34. The Bible tells us exactly when the Feast of Sukkot begins. Do you know? Each number below represents a letter of the alphabet (A = 1, B = 2, etc.). Replace each number with its letter to find out what Leviticus 23:34 says about this Appointed Time.

A	B	C	D	E	F	G	H	I	J	K	L	M
1	2	3	4	5	6	7	8	9	10	11	12	13
N	O	P	Q	R	S	T	U	V	W	X	Y	Z
14	15	16	17	18	19	20	21	22	23	24	25	26

1 15 – 14: _____

2 20 – 8 – 5: _____

3 6 – 9 – 6 – 20 – 5 – 5 – 14 – 20 – 8: _____

4 4 – 1 – 25: _____

5 15 – 6: _____

6 20 – 8 – 5: _____

7 19 – 5 – 22 – 5 – 14 – 20 – 8: _____

8 13 – 15 – 14 – 20 – 8: _____

Building the
TABERNACLE

Read Exodus 26:1-31:18. Answer the questions below.

(1) Who was the first high priest?

(2) What was the purpose of the tabernacle?

(3) Where was the mercy seat located?

(4) What was the mercy seat made of?

(5) Priests were chosen from which tribe of Israel?

(6) Which two men were put in charge of building the tabernacle?

(7) In which book of the Torah can you find instructions for building the tabernacle?

(8) What oil was used to keep the lamps burning in the tabernacle?

(9) What was the purpose of the brazen altar?

(10) The ark of the covenant was made from which type of wood?

God asked the Israelites to bring gifts to build the tabernacle. Read Exodus 25:1-9. Draw a selection of the gifts that the Israelites brought to contribute to the building of the tabernacle. Write the name of each gift below your drawing.

The tabernacle

The Israelites made special furniture for the tabernacle.
Cut out the furniture and place them in the tabernacle.

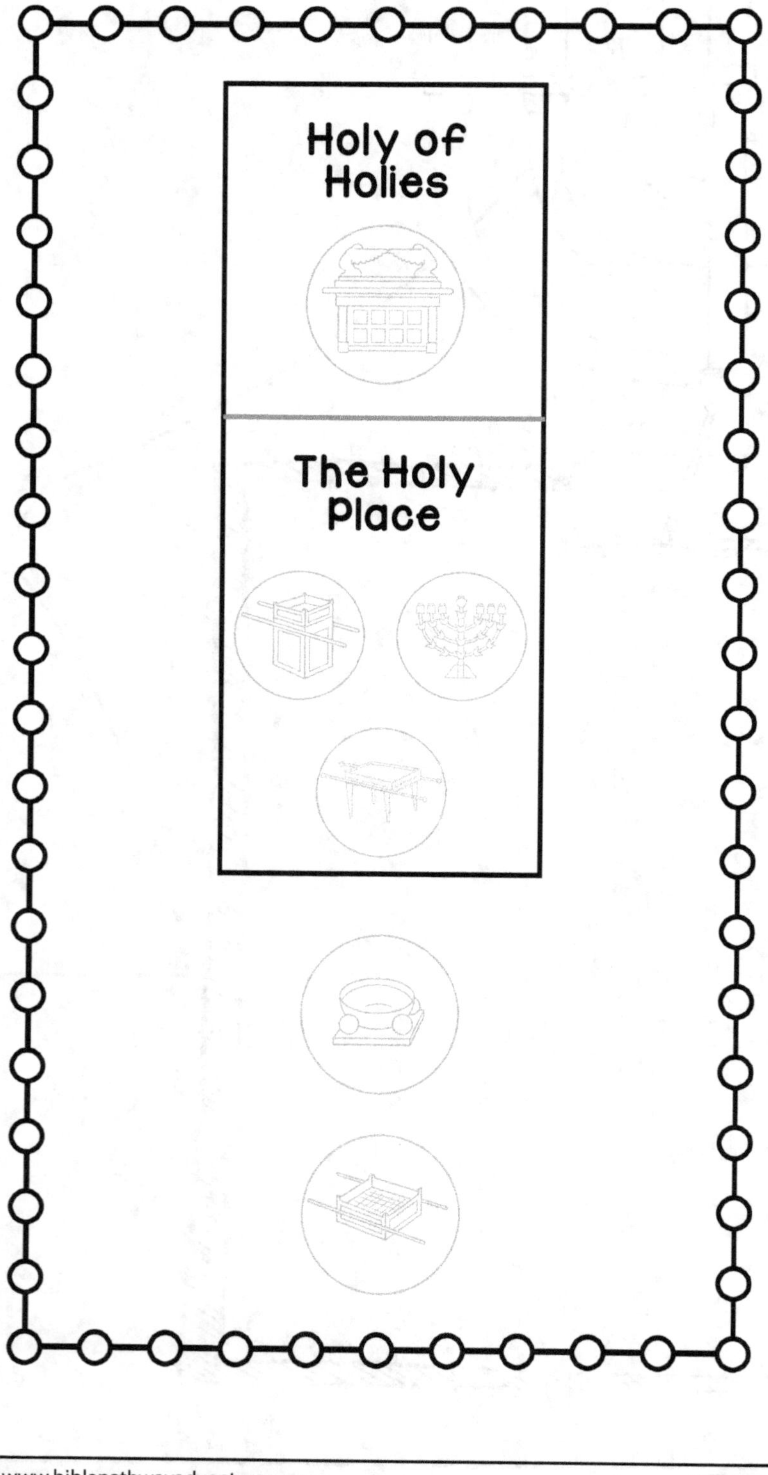

Holy of Holies

The Holy Place

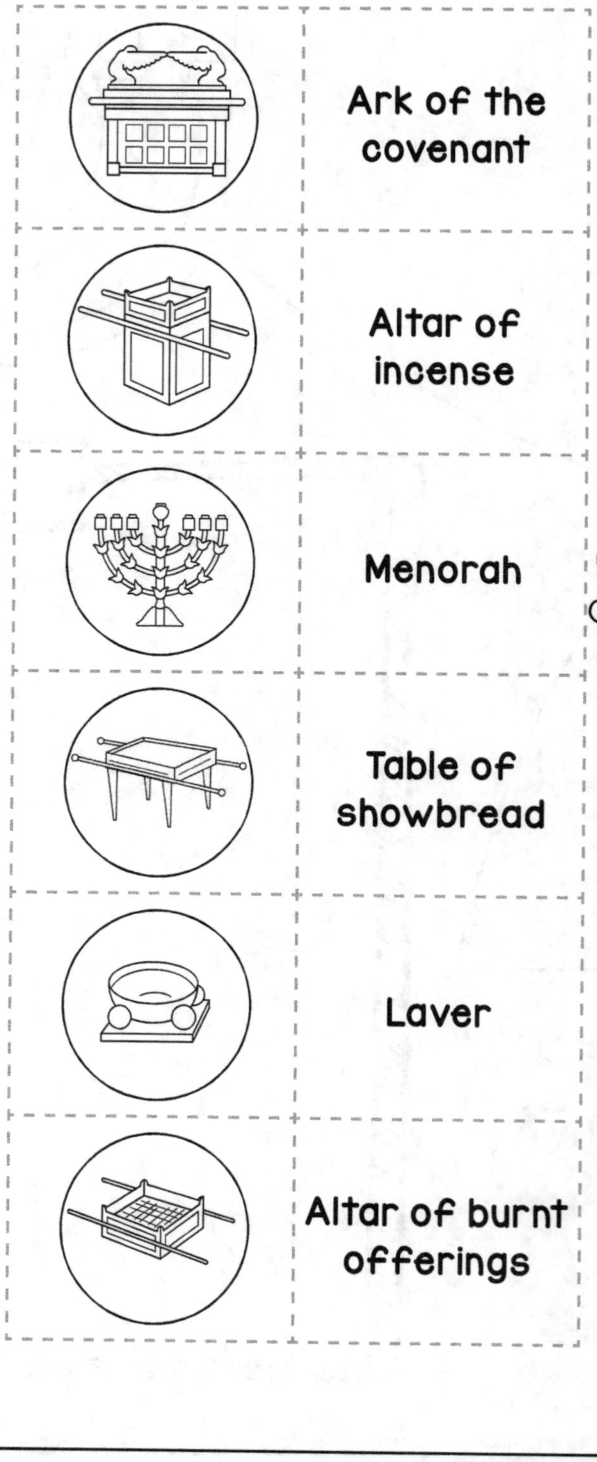

	Ark of the covenant
	Altar of incense
	Menorah
	Table of showbread
	Laver
	Altar of burnt offerings

The tabernacle

The tabernacle was a sacred place where Yah met the Israelites during the forty years they lived in the desert. It represented His throne on the earth and symbolized His dwelling among His people. It was here the Israelites came together to worship Yah and offer sacrifices. The tabernacle was a tent-like structure covered by animal skins surrounded by a white linen fence. The tabernacle itself was divided into two places – the Holy Place and the Holy of Holies – and only the priests could enter these areas. All the furniture in the Holy Place was made of gold, just as Yah instructed.

It was the job of the Levites to carry the tabernacle and set it up wherever the Israelites pitched camp. When the Levites erected the tabernacle, they placed it in the center of the camp. Moses, Aaron, and the priests camped on the east side next to the entrance, and the other tribes of Israel were grouped into four camps around the tabernacle's outer fence.

Read Exodus 26:1-31:18. Answer the questions below.

1. What was the purpose of the tabernacle?

2. Which two men were put in charge of building the tabernacle?

3. What oil was used to keep the lamps burning in the tabernacle?

4. What was the purpose of the brazen altar?

5. Where was the mercy seat located?

After the Israelites built the Tabernacle in the wilderness, they dedicated it to Yah. For twelve days, each tribe brought gifts. Imagine you are a member of one of the twelve tribes of Israel. Read Numbers 7:1–8:26, and complete the worksheet below.

TABERNACLE GIFTS

WHAT DID MOSES DO?	WHAT DID YOUR TRIBE DO?	YAH'S INSTRUCTIONS
....	....	....
....	....	....
....	....	....
....	....	....
....	....	....
....	....	....
....	....	....

Tribal offerings

In the wilderness, each of the twelve tribes of Israel brought an offering for the dedication of the altar. Read Numbers 7 and fill in the chart with the tribe's name and a summary of its offerings.

DAY 1

Tribe: ....

Gifts: ....

....

....

DAY 2

Tribe: ....

Gifts: ....

....

....

DAY 3

Tribe: ....

Gifts: ....

....

....

DAY 4

Tribe: ....

Gifts: ....

....

....

DAY 5

Tribe: ....

Gifts: ....

....

....

DAY 6

Tribe: ....

Gifts: ....

....

....

DAY 7

Tribe: ....

Gifts: ....

....

....

DAY 8

Tribe: ....

Gifts: ....

....

....

DAY 9

Tribe: ....

Gifts: ....

....

....

DAY 10

Tribe: ....

Gifts: ....

....

....

DAY 11

Tribe: ....

Gifts: ....

....

....

DAY 12

Tribe: ....

Gifts: ....

....

....

Match the tribal leaders

Read Numbers 7. Each tribal leader brought offerings before Yah.
Draw a line to match each tribe with its leader.
Then, draw a tribal offering in the space below.

TRIBE	LEADER
1. Judah	Eliasaph
2. Issachar	Abidan
3. Zebulun	Nethanel
4. Reuben	Pagiel
5. Simeon	Elizur
6. Gad	Nahshon
7. Ephraim	Gamaliel
8. Manasseh	Shelumiel
9. Benjamin	Elishama
10. Dan	Ahiezer
11. Asher	Eliab
12. Naphtali	Ahira

Draw a tribal offering.

Holy of Holies

The room known as the Holy of Holies was the most sacred area of the tabernacle (and the future temple in Jerusalem). It was separated from the rest of the tabernacle by the veil, a heavy curtain made of fine linen and blue, purple, and scarlet yarn, embroidered with gold cherubim. No one could enter except the High Priest, and even he could only enter once a year on the Day of Atonement (Yom Kippur) to offer the blood of sacrifice and the incense before the mercy seat. By doing this, the High Priest atoned for his own sins and the sins of the people. This was a foreshadowing of Yeshua, who would become the High Priest for all.

The Holy of Holies contained the Ark of the Covenant, made from pure gold with two cherubim guarding the mercy seat. Inside were the two stone tablets inscribed with God's commandments, Aaron's budded almond rod (Numbers 17:8), and a pot of manna (Hebrews 9:4). The Ark was covered with a lid made of pure gold (Exodus 37:6), known as the "mercy seat."

1. Read Leviticus 23. What did God instruct the Israelites to do each year on the Day of Atonement (Yom Kippur)?

    ....

    ....

2. Find two Bible verses in Exodus 25 that mention the mercy seat.

    ....

    ....

Ark of the Covenant

Read Exodus 25:1-22. This Bible passage describes the measurements for the ark and mercy seat. Fill in the blank spaces below. Color the ark.

Measurements for the mercy seat:

.... long

.... wide

Measurements for the ark:

.... long

.... wide

.... high

The ark and poles were made of ....

The ark and poles were overlaid with ....

The rings, lid of atonement and cherubim were made of ....

There were .... cherubim, ... rings, and .... poles.

The .... placed inside the ark.

Bible Pathway Adventures

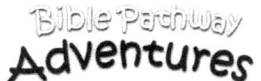

"Yah set apart the tribe of Levi to bear the ark of Yah's covenant..."

(Deuteronomy 10:8)

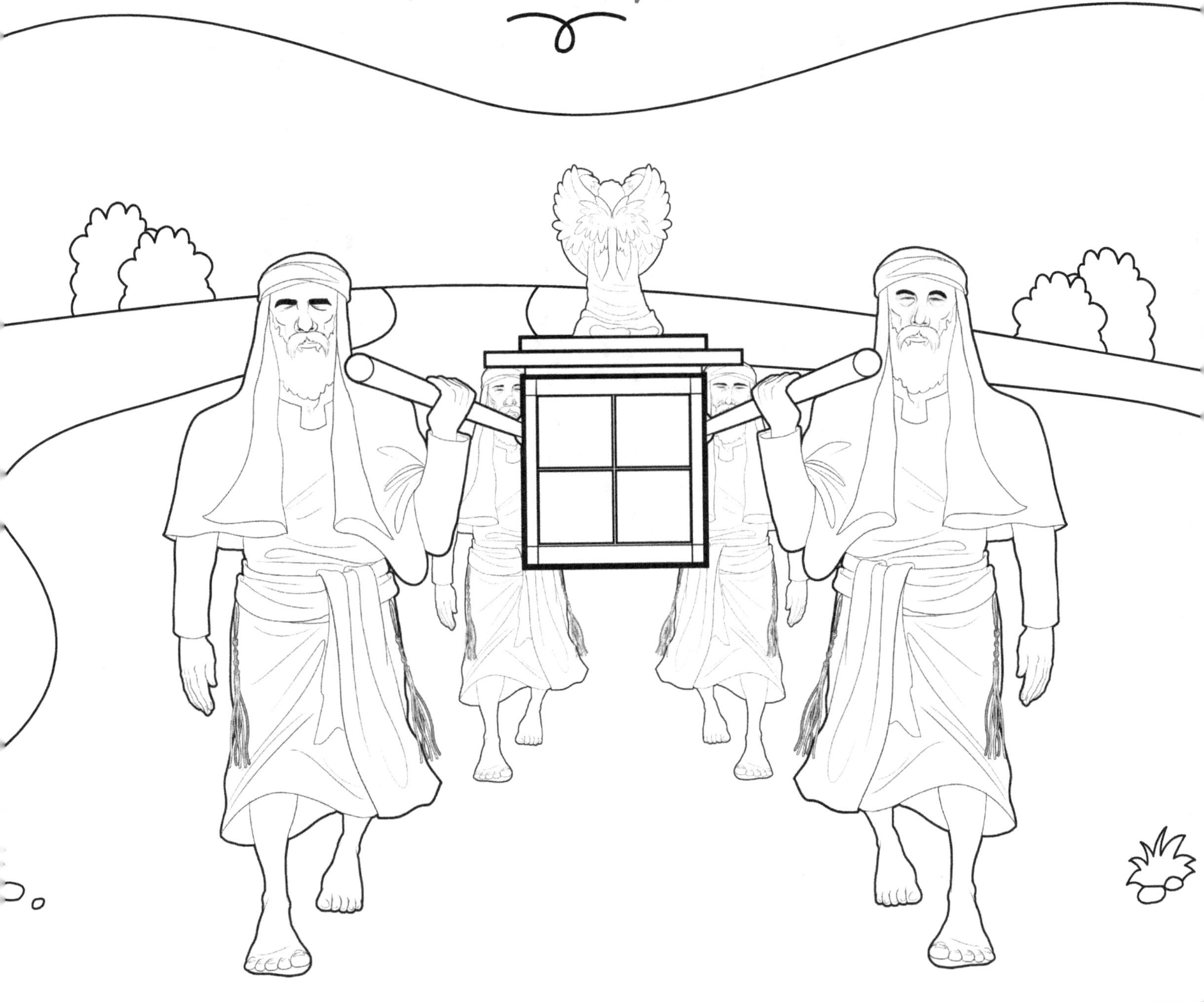

Yah appointed Aaron as the first high priest of the Israelites. Unscramble the words to learn more about the holy garments worn by Aaron.

AARON!

terapsBaelt ....

hepdo ....

ebro ....

etfitd nciut ....

anbtru ....

shas ....

nline ....

xyon tesson ....

✳ Read about the garments of the Israelite priests in Exodus 28:1-43.

The high priest's breastplate

Exodus 28 describes the high priest's breastplate.
Read this chapter and answer the questions below.

Label the following:

(a) chains of pure gold (2)
(b) rings (4)
(c) braided chains of
      corded work (2)
(d) settings of stones (12)

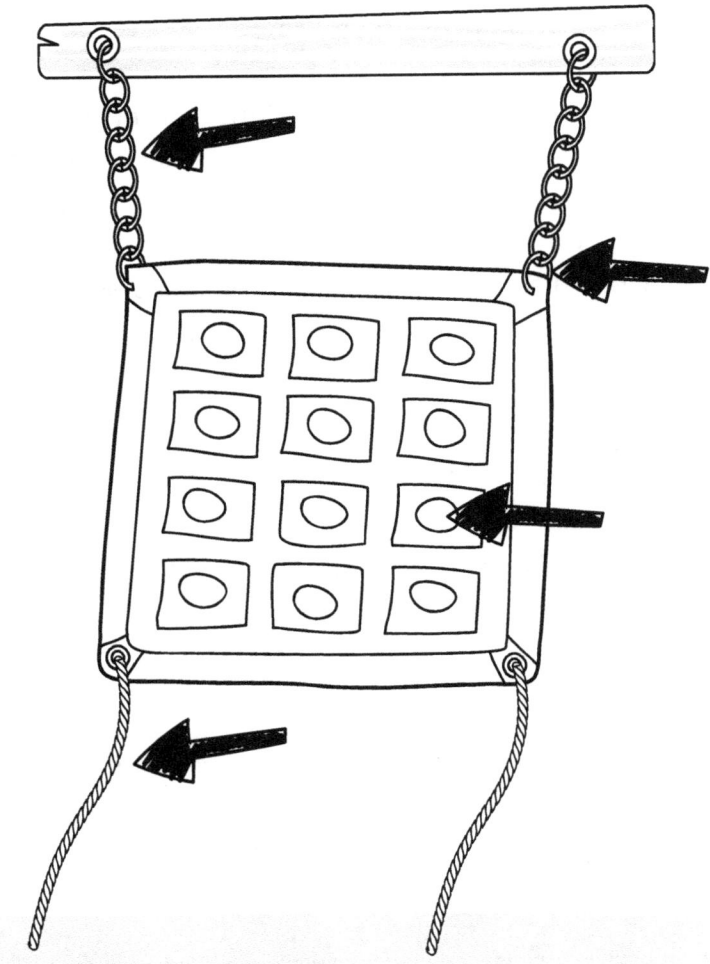

What was the breastplate made from?

1. ....   4. ....

2. ....   5. ....

3. ....

What metal were the chains made from? v 14

....

What shape was the breastplate? v 16

....

What was written on each stone? v 21

....

PRUSSIAN BLUE

The high priest's garments were woven with a deep, rich blue thread. This special color, known today as Prussian blue, was made from a mixture of ash and blood, which came from the animal sacrifices, and a chemical called cyanide, which can be found in almond seeds.

Some people wonder if this same color might be used again in the future. Could Yeshua, who is also our High Priest, use the sacred items found in the Ark of the Covenant, like the almond branch, stone tablets, and manna, along with His own blood, to prepare the garments He will wear when He returns to reign on earth? "Then I saw a Lamb, looking as if it had been slain, standing at the center of the throne..." *(Revelation 5:6)*

Answer the questions.

1. What is Prussian Blue, and how was it made?

   ....

   ....

2. Why do you think the high priest wore this color?

   ....

   ....

3. What items were placed inside the Ark of the Covenant?

   ....

   ....

Trace and draw the high priest's robe. Remember to include a breastplate, a sash, and the golden bells.

Spies into Canaan

Moses sent twelve spies, one from each tribe of Israel, to explore the land of Canaan. When the men came back, they gave different reports. Read Numbers 13–14. Decide which statements show faith and which show fear. Write each statement in the correct box below, include who said it, and then explain why you think each one shows faith or fear.

Faith

Fear

We can't fight them.

They are stronger than us.

Let us choose a leader and go back to Egypt.

We felt like grasshoppers next to them.

The land we explored is good. We can do it!

If Yah is pleased with us, He will give us the land.

Do not fear the people of the land.

Giants in the land

According to the Bible, there were giants called the Nephilim, who were known for being very large and strong but also violent and wicked (Genesis 6:1-4). Some were so massive they could grow up to twenty feet tall! Skeletons found in places like France and California suggest how tall they might have been, with some even having double rows of teeth or six fingers and toes. The most famous giant in the Bible was Goliath, who stood over nine feet tall. His armor was so heavy that just his coat weighed more than 150 pounds!
Read Genesis 6 and Numbers 13, then answer the questions.

1. Who were the Nephilim, and where did the spies say they saw them?

....

....

2. How did the spies' report about the Nephilim change the Israelites' plans?

....

....

3. What did Caleb and Joshua say about the land of Canaan, even though there were Nephilim there?

....

....

Korah
REBELS

Read Numbers 16:1-50. Complete the crossword below.

ACROSS

3) "Depart from the _____ of these wicked men and touch nothing of theirs…"

6) A _____ came into the camp and killed 14,700 people.

7) "You have gone too far, sons of _____!"

8) Korah went before Moses with Dathan, On, and _____.

9) Korah challenged the authority of _____ and Moses.

10) All the people who belonged to Korah went down alive to _____.

DOWN

1) The cloud covered the tent of _____ and the glory of God appeared.

2) All the _____ of Israel grumbled against Moses and Aaron.

4) The earth opened its mouth and _____ them up.

5) "_____ yourselves from among this congregation…"

The complaining Israelites

Korah, Dathan, Abiram, and 250 other leaders of the Israelites believed that Moses and Aaron were acting as if they were more important than everyone else. They came to Moses and Aaron to complain about their leadership. Read Numbers 16:1-14 and write what the rebels said to them during these conversations. Complete the activity by adding facial expressions to the men and labeling them with their names.

Aaron's staff
BUDS

Read Numbers 17:1-13. Answer the questions below.

1. "Speak to the _____ __ ____, and get from them staffs, one for each fathers' house."

2. What instructions did God give Moses about the staffs?

3. Whose name was written on the staff for the tribe of Levi?

4. How many staffs were brought to the tabernacle?

5. What miracle happened to Aaron's staff overnight?

6. What did the budding of Aaron's staff prove to the Israelites?

7. Where did Aaron's staff bud?

8. Where did God tell Moses to place Aaron's staff after it budded?

9. Why was Aaron's staff placed before the Ark of the Covenant?

10. What lesson did you learn from the story of Aaron's staff?

House of Levi

The story of Aaron's staff budding shows how Yah proved to the Israelites that He had chosen Aaron to be the high priest. Read Numbers 17:1-13 and tell the story in your own words. Then complete the picture.

....
....
....
....
....
....
....
....

Who was Balaam?

Read Numbers 22:1-25:9 and 31:1-54. Complete the worksheet below.

Balaam is most famous for:

....

King Balak asked Balaam to:

....

The angel of God told Balaam:

....

Balaam blessed Israel:

1. ....

2. ....

3. ....

To defeat the Israelites, Balaam told the Moabites to:

....

....

Spiritual adultery

In the Bible, Yah compared the people of Israel to a young wife, raised up to honor Him as her husband through a covenant. He gave the Israelites clear instructions to follow, but throughout the Old Testament (Tanakh), they often disobeyed. Instead of staying faithful to Yah, the Israelites followed the ungodly practices of their neighbors, like the Canaanites (Numbers 25:1–9). The same rituals and customs that the pagans used to worship false gods were used by the Israelites to worship Yah, the true God. Yah compared this behavior to a disloyal wife committing adultery, calling it spiritual unfaithfulness.

Have you ever wondered why Yah was unhappy with Balaam? Balaam taught King Balak how to trap the men of Israel into sinning against Yah (Numbers 31:16). He told the king to send Canaanite women who worshiped other gods to tempt the Israelites. Balaam knew that if the men followed these women and their false worship, they would forget Yah's commands. Without obedience, the Israelites would grow weak and be defeated.

1. How did the Israelites commit spiritual adultery?

....

2. How can you commit spiritual adultery today?

....

3. Read James 4:4. Write the scripture below.

....

....

DID YOU KNOW?

Why Moses Couldn't Enter the Promised Land

Moses led the Israelites through the wilderness for 40 years. But when they finally reached the edge of the Promised Land, Yah did not allow him to enter. Why? Earlier, at a place called Meribah, the Israelites were thirsty and began to complain. Yah told Moses to speak to the rock so that water would come out. But instead, Moses said, "Hear now, you rebels: shall we bring water for you out of this rock?" Then he struck the rock twice with his staff. Yah was not pleased because Moses did not honor Him as holy (set-apart) in front of the Israelites. Yah said, "Because you did not believe in Me, to uphold Me as holy in the eyes of the people of Israel, therefore you shall not bring this assembly into the land that I have given them" (Numbers 20:12).

Moses climbed Mount Nebo. From there, Yah showed him the land the Israelites would soon enter. Then Moses died in the land of Moab. He was 120 years old.

God chose Joshua to lead the Israelites across the Jordan River into the Promised Land.

NUMBERS 27

THINK ABOUT IT

Why do you think Yah chose Joshua to lead
the Israelites into the Promised Land?

....

....

A faithful leader

Read Exodus 1, 24; Numbers 13-14, 27; Deuteronomy 1, 34;
Joshua 1, 6, 11, 24, and the article below. Answer the question.

Joshua was born in the land of Egypt during a time when the Israelites were slaves (Exodus 1:13-14). He was from the tribe of Ephraim, one of the 12 tribes of Israel (Numbers 13:8). As a young man, he became an assistant to Moses, the leader Yah chose to free the Israelites from slavery. During the Israelites' 40 years of wandering in the wilderness, Joshua stayed loyal to Moses. He followed Yah faithfully and was one of the only people who trusted Yah's promise to give the Israelites the Promised Land (Deuteronomy 1:36-38).

When Moses sent twelve spies to explore the land of Canaan (Numbers 13:1-3), Joshua and Caleb were the only two who believed that Yah would help them conquer it (Numbers 14:6-9). Because of their faith, Yah said Joshua and Caleb would live to see the Promised Land, while many others would not (Numbers 14:30). While Moses was still alive, Yah told him to appoint Joshua as the next leader of Israel (Numbers 27:18-23). Moses laid his hands on Joshua in front of the people, showing that Yah had chosen him (Deuteronomy 34:9). After Moses died, Joshua led the Israelites into the Promised Land (Joshua 1:1-2). With Yah's guidance, he led many battles to defeat the nations living there (Joshua 11:23). At the end of his life, Joshua told the people, "Choose this day whom you will serve... But as for me and my house, we will serve Yahweh" (Joshua 24:15).

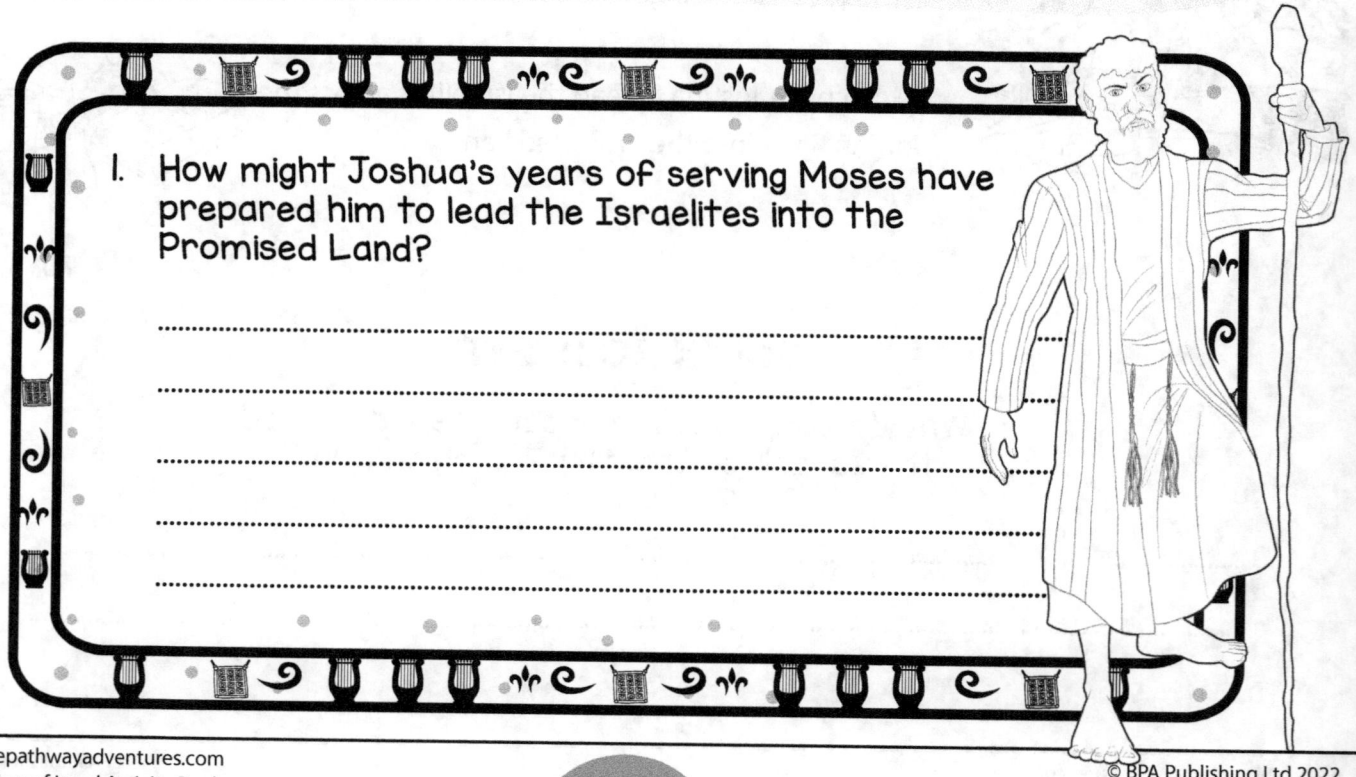

I. How might Joshua's years of serving Moses have prepared him to lead the Israelites into the Promised Land?

....

....

....

....

....

Joshua and the Promised Land

Rahab hides the spies

Read Joshua 2:8-24 (ESV). Using the words below,
fill in the blanks to complete the Bible passage.

BUSINESS	HOUSE	ROPE	RED SEA	KINDLY	HEAVENS
WATER	EGYPT	JORDAN	FATHER	INHABITANTS	SPIRIT

" Before the men lay down, Rahab came up to them on the roof and said, "I know that God has given you the land, and that the fear of you has fallen upon us, and that all the .... of the land melt away before you. We have heard how God dried up the .... of the .... before you when you came out of ...., and what you did to the two kings of the Amorites who were beyond the ...., to Sihon and Og, whom you devoted to destruction. As soon as we heard it, our hearts melted, and there was no .... left in any man because of you, for Elohim your God, he is God in the .... above and on the earth beneath. Please swear to me by the Lord that, as I have dealt kindly with you, you also will deal .... with my father's ...., and give me a sure sign that you will save alive my .... and mother, my brothers and sisters, and all who belong to them, and deliver our lives from death." The men said to her, "Our life for yours even to death! If you do not tell this .... of ours, then when God gives us the land we will deal kindly and faithfully with you." Then Rahab let them down by a .... through the window. "

The Jordan River

The Israelites crossed the Jordan River into Canaan so they could enter the Promised Land. Using the internet or an encyclopedia, complete the worksheet below.

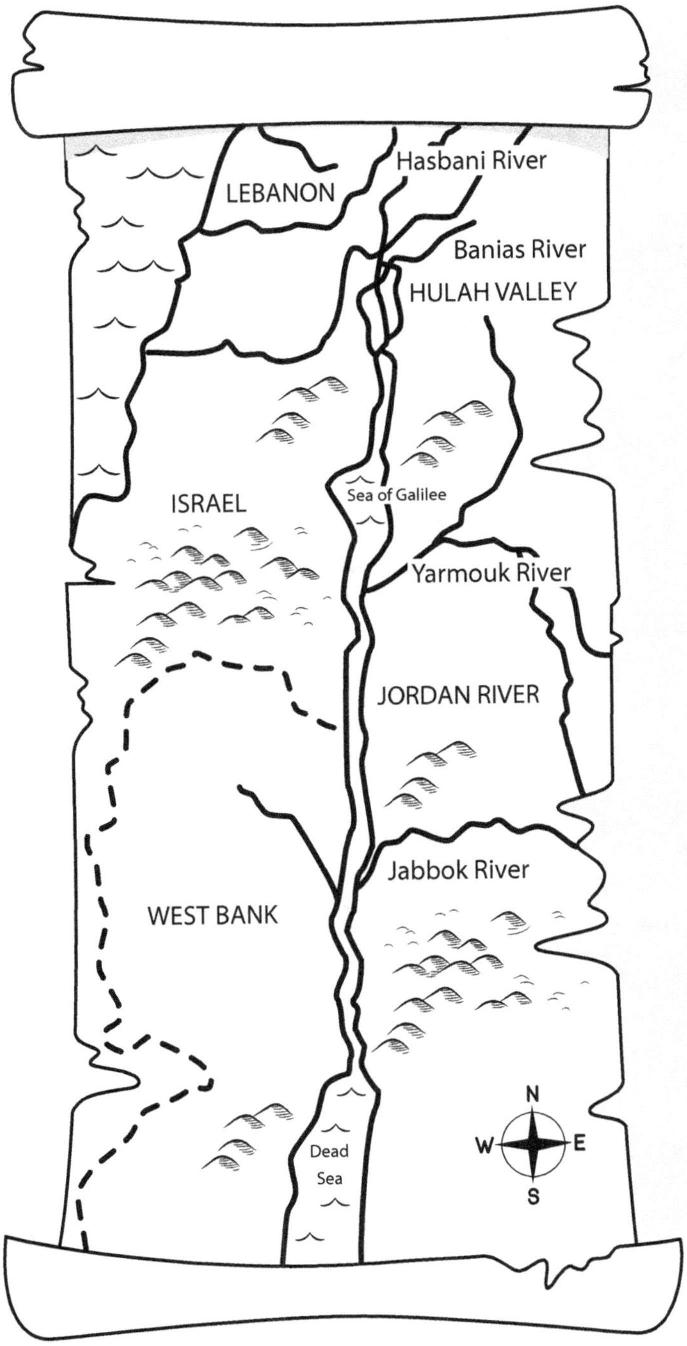

Length:

....

Starts:

....

Location:

....

Direction it flows:

....

Where it empties:

....

Importance of the Jordan Valley to ancient Israel:

....

Two famous Bible stories that mention this river:

....

....

Map labels: Hasbani River, LEBANON, Banias River, HULAH VALLEY, ISRAEL, Sea of Galilee, Yarmouk River, JORDAN RIVER, Jabbok River, WEST BANK, Dead Sea, N W E S

Pesach

The Hebrew name for Passover is Pesach. Before the Israelites left Egypt, they ate a meal of lamb, unleavened bread, and bitter herbs. This meal was part of God's plan to protect them from the final plague. Each year, they were to observe the Passover meal to remind them of how God delivered them from slavery in Egypt and brought them to freedom. When the Israelites entered the Promised Land, they kept their first Passover in Canaan while camped at Gilgal (Joshua 5:10-12).

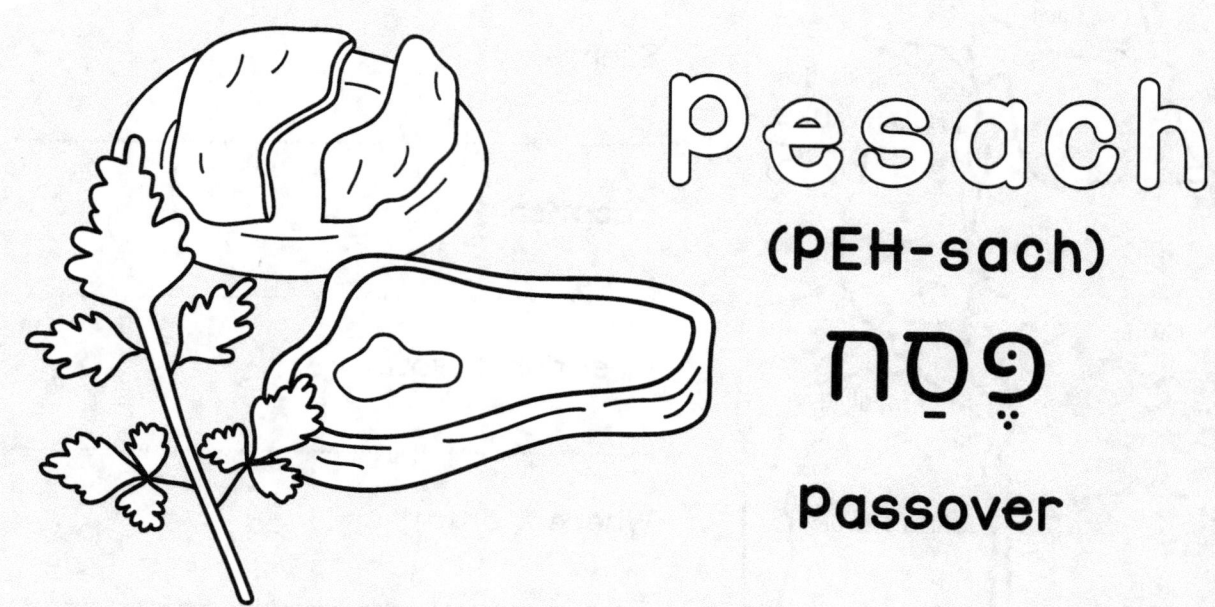

Pesach
(PEH-sach)
פֶּסַח
Passover

Trace the Hebrew name here:

פֶּסַח

פֶּסַח

Write the Hebrew name here:

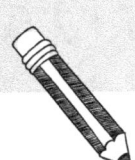
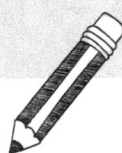

Let's write!

Practice writing 'Pesach' on the lines below.

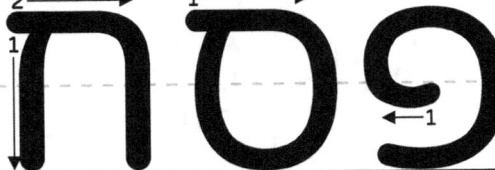

פסח

Try this on your own.
Remember that Hebrew is read from RIGHT to LEFT.

Why did the Israelites keep the Passover on the fourteenth day of the month?

....

....

....

....

Israel crosses the Jordan

Read Joshua 3:1-17. When the priests stepped into the Jordan River, something amazing happened. This miracle helped the Israelites cross into the Promised Land. Do you know what it was? Each number below represents a letter of the alphabet (A = 1, B = 2, etc.). Replace each number with its letter to reveal the miracle.

A	B	C	D	E	F	G	H	I	J	K	L	M
1	2	3	4	5	6	7	8	9	10	11	12	13
N	O	P	Q	R	S	T	U	V	W	X	Y	Z
14	15	16	17	18	19	20	21	22	23	24	25	26

1 20 – 8 – 5: _____

2 23 – 1 – 20 – 5 – 18: _____

3 19 – 20 – 15 – 16 – 16 – 5 – 4: _____

4 6 – 12 – 15 – 23 – 9 – 14 – 7: _____

5 1 – 14 – 4: _____

6 20 – 8 – 5: _____

7 18 – 9 – 22 – 5 – 18: _____

8 16 – 1 – 18 – 20 – 5 – 4: _____

"Be strong and courageous, for you shall cause this people to inherit the land that I swore to their fathers to give them."

(Joshua 1:6)

Battle instructions

Read Joshua 5:13-6:5. As Joshua stood near Jericho, he spotted a Man with a sword in His hand. Full of courage, Joshua asked, "Are you for us or our enemies?" The Man replied, "I am the Commander of Yah's army." Realizing this was no ordinary warrior, Joshua fell to the ground in worship. "Take off your sandals," the Commander said, "This is holy (set-apart) ground." Meanwhile, Jericho's gates were shut tight. But Yah gave Joshua a strange command—march around the city once each day for six days. On the seventh day, seven priests would blow shofars, and after a mighty shout, the walls would fall.

1. What did the Commander of Yah's army tell Joshua to do?

   ....

   ....

2. Why do you think Yah used this battle plan instead of attacking Jericho directly?

   ....

   ....

God's Battle Plan for
JERICHO

Read Joshua 6:1-7. God gave Joshua a special plan to capture Jericho.
Write in each box what happened each day.

DAY 1	DAY 2	DAY 3	DAY 4	DAY 5	DAY 6	DAY 7
March once, carry shofars and ark						

Battle of Jericho

Read Joshua 6:15-20. What happened on the seventh day?

....
....
....
....
....
....
....
....
....

Why do you think Joshua made an oath, cursing anyone who rebuilds Jericho?

....
....
....
....
....
....
....
....

What happened to Rahab and her family?

....
....
....
....
....
....

If the battle of Jericho was a book, the cover would look like this...

Battle of Jericho

Read Joshua 6:1-27 and review the ten sentences below. They recount the story of the battle of Jericho, but they're out of order! Your task is to arrange the sentences in the correct order by writing a number next to each sentence.

A. .... When the people heard the sound of the shofar (trumpet), they shouted loudly and the wall fell flat.

B. .... On the second day, they marched around the city once and returned to their camp. They did this for six days.

C. .... They destroyed everything living in Jericho – the people, cattle, sheep, and donkeys.

D. .... They put all the silver, gold, and bronze and iron items into the treasury of God's house.

E. .... At that time, Joshua made them take an oath.

F. .... The men rescued Rahab and her family.

G. .... Joshua told the priests, "Carry the Ark of the Covenant. Seven priests should carry shofars and march in front of it."

H. .... Joshua told the people, "March around the city, and let the armed soldiers walk in front of the Ark of the Covenant."

I. .... On the seventh day, they woke up at dawn and marched around the city seven times.

J. .... God told Joshua, "I have given you Jericho, along with its king and mighty warriors."

Battle of Ai

The Israelites first attacked the city of Ai but were defeated because Achan had disobeyed Yah by keeping things from Jericho that were meant to be destroyed. What happened next? Read Joshua 7:1-8:29. Answer the questions below.

How did the Israelites act unfaithfully?

....

Why did the Israelites lose the first war with Ai?

....

What was Israel's strategy to overtake the city of Ai?

....

What instructions did Yah give to Joshua during the battle of Ai?

....

What was the outcome of Israel's battle with Ai?

....

JOSHUA READS THE COVENANT

After a tough battle and a lesson about obeying Yah's commands, Joshua led the Israelites to a place called Mount Ebal. There, he built an altar using stones that had not been shaped by tools, just as Moses had commanded. The Israelites offered burnt offerings and peace offerings to thank Yah. Then, Joshua copied all the words of the Torah onto stones so everyone could read them.

 ## BLESSINGS AND CURSES

All the Israelites stood together with the foreigners living among them. Half the people stood in front of Mount Gerizim, and the other half faced Mount Ebal. Joshua read aloud every word of the covenant, including the blessings and the curses. Read Joshua 7:1-8:35 and answer the questions below.

 ## THINK ABOUT IT

1. Why do you think Joshua built an altar on Mount Ebal?

   ....

2. What did Joshua write on the stones?

   ....

3. Read Deuteronomy 28:1-68. List five blessings and five curses that Yah promises the House of Israel if they obey or disobey His commands.

   ....

   ....

   ....

   ....

Gibeonites deceive the Israelites

The Gibeonites heard how Joshua and the Israelites had defeated Jericho and Ai. Fearing for their lives, they used a clever trick to make a covenant with Israel. Use what you know from Joshua 9:1-27 to answer the questions.

True or False?

The Gibeonites pretended to be travelers from a faraway country.　　◯ **True** ◯ **False**

Before making a covenant with the Gibeonites, Joshua asked Yah for guidance.　　◯ **True** ◯ **False**

The Israelites were told to kill the Gibeonites for their deception.　　◯ **True** ◯ **False**

The Gibeonites brought fresh bread and clean clothes to trick Joshua.　　◯ **True** ◯ **False**

The leaders of Israel swore an oath to let the Gibeonites live.　　◯ **True** ◯ **False**

The Gibeonites became woodcutters and water carriers for the congregation and the altar of Yah.　　◯ **True** ◯ **False**

The sun stands STILL

Read Joshua 10:1-28. Find and circle the words below.

```
P  C  T  U  C  Y  J  E  Q  S  D  M  A  I  A
O  P  P  M  A  B  Y  P  S  U  U  H  D  S  V
M  O  O  N  M  Z  Z  W  X  E  I  R  O  R  D
S  O  H  C  A  W  V  T  M  L  U  N  N  A  N
G  Z  A  G  I  U  Q  I  M  X  X  H  I  E  W
V  F  I  D  J  Q  A  W  B  F  L  F  Z  L  D
K  Y  L  T  A  F  V  T  F  U  N  N  E  R  E
G  T  S  H  L  K  N  Y  T  K  V  V  D  G  F
I  F  T  T  O  T  F  E  J  A  K  W  E  I  E
B  H  O  Q  N  O  Z  K  F  L  C  R  K  L  A
E  B  N  G  L  W  S  N  T  M  S  K  H  G  T
O  U  E  L  A  V  U  U  S  T  L  S  V  A  K
N  Q  S  P  Q  P  N  K  W  E  P  I  Q  L  Z
A  M  O  R  I  T  E  K  I  N  G  S  S  Z  C
L  V  I  C  T  O  R  Y  A  E  O  B  X  R  Q
```

GILGAL

ATTACK

SUN

DEFEAT

AMORITE KINGS

MOON

AIJALON

VICTORY

HAILSTONES

ISRAEL

GIBEON

ADONIZEDEK

Cities of REFUGE

Read Numbers 35:1-34. Answer the questions below.

(1) Where were the Israelites camped when God spoke to Moses?

(2) Who did God command the Israelites to give cities to?

(3) What did the Levites use the cities and pastures for?

(4) How many cities in total were the Israelites to give to the Levites?

(5) What were the six special cities called?

(6) Why were the cities of refuge important?

(7) Who could flee to a city of refuge?

(8) How long could someone stay in a city of refuge?

(9) What was the difference between murder and accidental killing, according to God's rules?

(10) What did God remind the Israelites about keeping the land holy (set-apart)?

Cities of Refuge

God gave the Israelites instructions to create six Cities of Refuge when they reached the land of Canaan. These cities were set aside as safe places for anyone who accidentally hurt or killed someone and needed protection. Read Numbers 35:1-34 and Joshua 20:1-9. Then, using the map, find the six Cities of Refuge and write their names in the correct locations. Afterward, discuss: Who was allowed to flee to a city of refuge, and how long could they stay there? Why do you think God created cities of refuge to handle accidental killings?

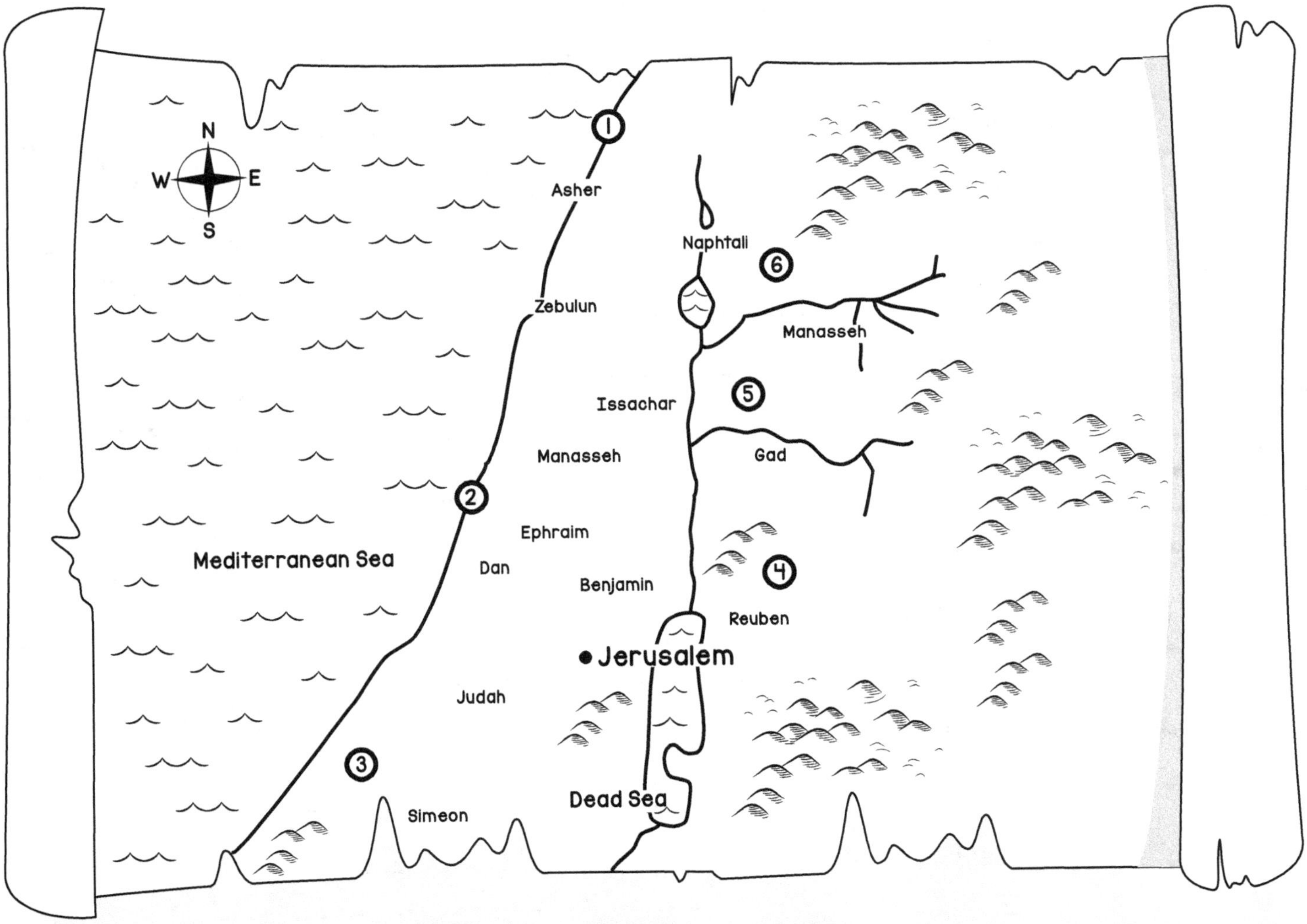

Asher
N W E S
Naphtali ⑥
Zebulun
Manasseh
Issachar
⑤
Manasseh
Gad
②
Ephraim
Mediterranean Sea
Dan
Benjamin
④
Reuben
●Jerusalem
Judah
③
Dead Sea
Simeon

KEDESH   HEBRON   RAMOTH
SHECHEM   BEZER   GOLAN

Tribal inheritance

Read Joshua 13:1-21:45. The Promised Land was divided among the twelve tribes of Israel. On the scroll below, write the land each tribe received beside its name.

BENJAMIN

DAN

LEVI

Reuben: ....

Gad: ....

Manasseh: ....

Judah: ....

Ephraim: ....

Benjamin: ....

Simeon: ....

Zebulun: ....

Issachar: ....

Asher: ....

Naphtali: ....

Dan: ....

Levi: ....

Altar of Witness

After helping the other tribes conquer the Promised Land, the tribes of Reuben, Gad, and the half-tribe of Manasseh returned to their land on the east side of the Jordan River. Before they crossed the river, they built a large altar near the Jordan. When the other Israelites saw the altar, they misunderstood. They thought it was a sign that the eastern tribes were turning away from Yah and starting false worship. The tribes gathered at Shiloh to go to war against their brothers. What happened next?

Read Joshua 22:1-34. What happened after the tribes gathered at Shiloh?

....

....

....

....

Draw a 4-panel comic about the story of the altar of witness. In each panel, draw a simple picture or symbol to show these events:

1. The tribes of Reuben, Gad, and the half-tribe of Manasseh build an altar near the Jordan River.
2. The western tribes see the altar and get ready to go to war.
3. Phinehas and ten leaders from the western tribes meet with the eastern tribes.
4. The leaders return from Gilead with good news that makes the Israelites happy.

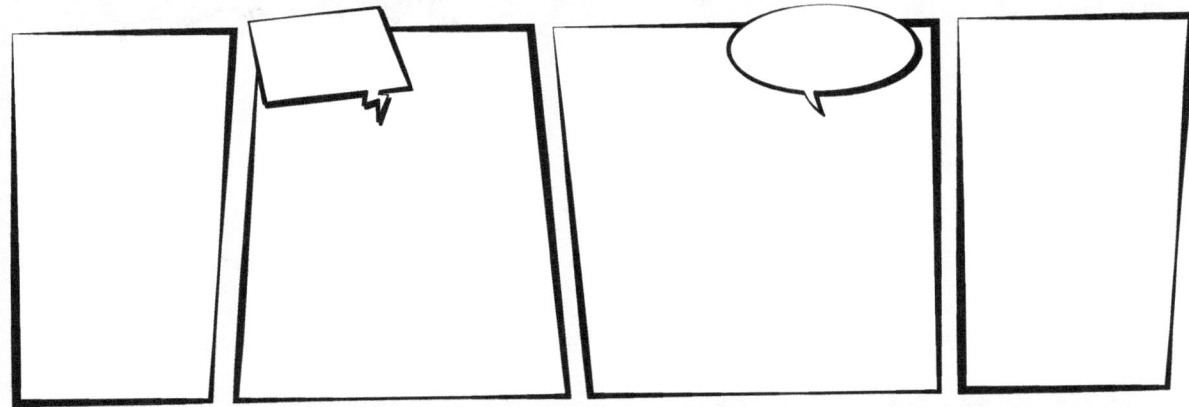

Bible Pathway Adventures

The promised land

Read Joshua 13:1-21:45. In the land of Canaan, each tribe was given a piece of land. Write the name of each tribe next to the matching number.

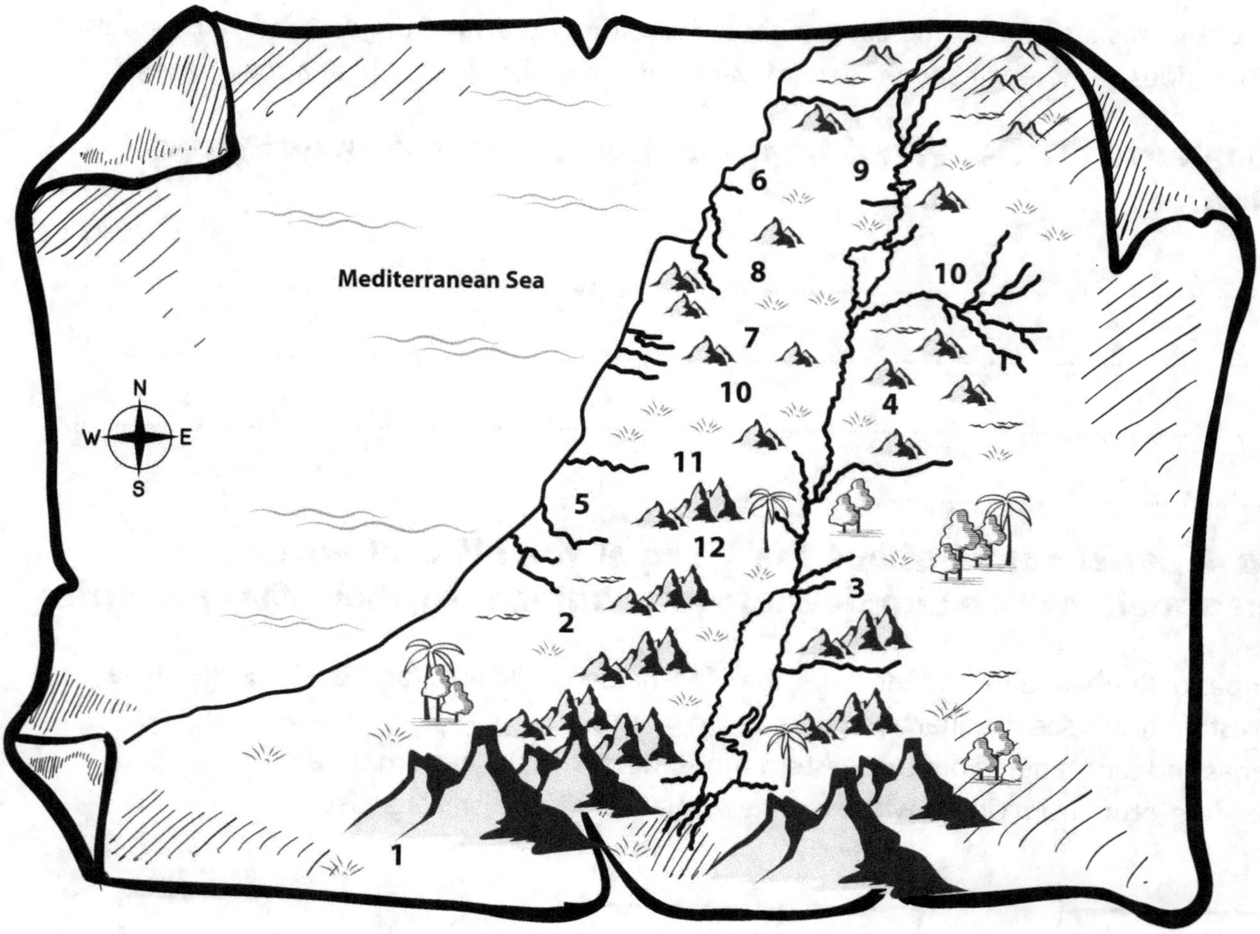
Mediterranean Sea
N
W
E
S
1
2
3
4
5
6
7
8
9
10
10
11
12

Simeon
Judah
Reuben
Gad
Dan
Asher
Issachar
Zebulun
Naphtali
Manasseh
Ephraim
Benjamin

1. ....
2. ....
3. ....
4. ....
5. ....
6. ....
7. ....
8. ....
9. ....
10. ....
11. ....
12. ....

"But as for me and my house, we will serve Yah."

(Joshua 24:15)

12 tribes of Israel

Worksheets

TRIBE OF REUBEN

 ## Tribal history

The Tribe of Reuben was named after Reuben, the oldest son of Jacob and Leah. As the firstborn, Reuben was supposed to receive the birthright, including leadership of the family and a double share of the inheritance. But Reuben made a serious mistake. In Genesis 35:22, he dishonored his father by lying with his father's concubine. Because of this, he lost his birthright, which was later given to Joseph's sons, Ephraim and Manasseh (1 Chronicles 5:1-2). In Genesis 49:3-4, Jacob gave blessings to each of his sons. To Reuben he said, "You are my firstborn… Unstable as water, you shall not have pre-eminence." Still, the tribe of Reuben played an important role in Israel's history.

TRIBE OF REUBEN

When the Israelites were getting ready to enter the Promised Land, the tribe of Reuben chose to live on the land east of the Jordan River. It was excellent for raising livestock (Numbers 32:1-5). Along with the tribes of Gad and half of Manasseh, they helped fight in the battles to take the land before returning home. In Joshua 22, they built an altar near the Jordan River. The other tribes feared it was for idol worship, but the tribe explained that it was a reminder that they still served Yah. Later, during the time of the Judges, the tribe of Reuben was criticized for staying with their flocks instead of joining the fight against Sisera (Judges 5:15-16).

 ## Answer the questions.

1. Why did Reuben lose his birthright from his father Jacob?

   ....

2. Where did the tribe of Reuben live when the Israelites entered the land?

   ....

3. What happened when the tribe of Reuben built an altar in Joshua 22?

   ....

4. What does Jacob's blessing tell you about Reuben and his tribe?

   ....

WHERE DID THE TRIBE OF REUBEN LIVE?

Read Numbers 32 and Joshua 13-15 to learn how the tribe of Reuben received their own piece of land in the Promised Land.

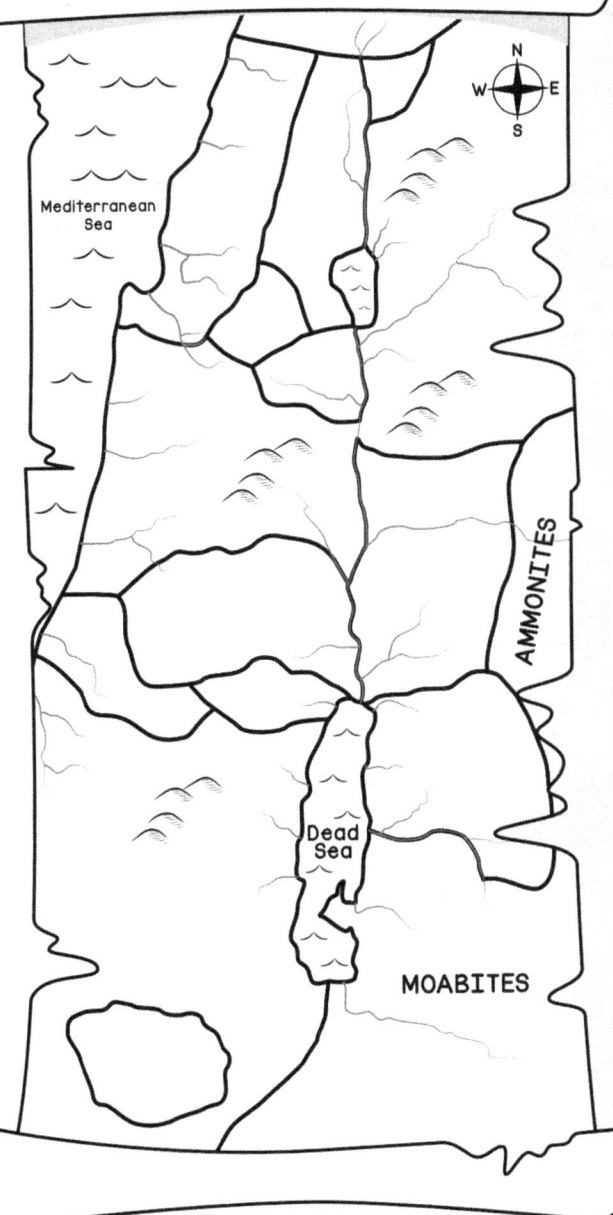

Land of Israel

Mediterranean Sea

AMMONITES

Dead Sea

MOABITES

Instructions:

1. Shade the area where the tribe of Reuben lived with blue.

2. Use a marker to trace the path of the Jordan River on your map.

3. Draw a sheep near the river to show that Reuben's tribe raised animals.

4. Write why the Jordan River was important to the tribe of Reuben.

....

....

....

....

Did You Know?

Reuben tried to save his brother Joseph when the others wanted to kill him. He told them to throw Joseph into a pit instead, because he planned to rescue him later (Genesis 37:21–22).

TRIBE OF SIMEON

 **Tribal history**

The Tribe of Simeon was named after Simeon, the second son of Jacob and Leah. In Genesis 34, he and his brother Levi attacked the city of Shechem to defend their sister Dinah. Although they were trying to protect their family, Jacob was upset with their actions and said they were too violent. Simeon also appears in the story of Joseph in Egypt. When Joseph's brothers came to Egypt to buy food during the famine, they didn't recognize him. To test them, Joseph kept Simeon in prison while the others returned home to bring back their youngest brother, Benjamin (Genesis 42:24).

TRIBE OF SIMEON

Later in Jacob's life, he gave blessings to each of his sons. In Genesis 49:5–7, Jacob warned that Simeon and Levi's anger would cause trouble. When the Israelites entered the Promised Land, the tribe of Simeon did not receive its own separate piece of land. Instead, their land was placed inside the territory of Judah. The people of Simeon were strong warriors. They helped the tribe of Judah in battles and supported David when he became king (1 Chronicles 12:25). Later, some families from Simeon traveled to the hill country of Seir to find more land for their flocks and herds.

 **Answer the questions.**

1. Why did Joseph keep Simeon in prison in Egypt?

   ....

2. What did Jacob say about Simeon and Levi in his blessing?

   ....

3. Where was the tribe of Simeon's land located?

   ....

4. How did the tribe of Simeon help King David?

   ....

WHERE DID THE TRIBE OF SIMEON LIVE?

Read Joshua 19:1–9 to learn how the tribe of Simeon received their land inside the territory of Judah.

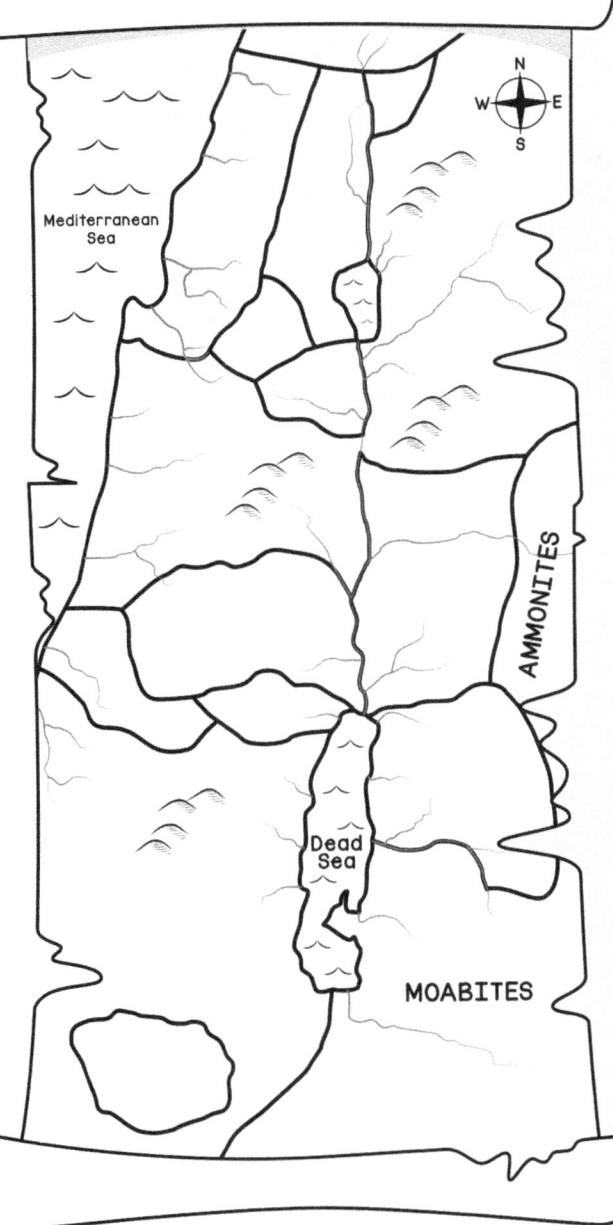

Land of Israel

Mediterranean Sea

AMMONITES

Dead Sea

MOABITES

Instructions:

1. Shade the area where the tribe of Simeon lived with green.

2. Use a black marker to outline the land of Judah, since Simeon's land was inside it.

3. Draw a city symbol to show that the tribe of Simeon lived in towns within Judah's territory.

4. Read Genesis 49:5-7. Why do you think Simeon's land different from the land of the other tribes?

....

....

....

Did You Know?

Simeon and his brother Levi attacked the city of Shechem to defend their sister Dinah (Genesis 34). Even though their actions were meant to protect, their father Jacob was not pleased.

TRIBE OF JUDAH

 **Tribal history**

The Tribe of Judah was named after Judah, the fourth son of Jacob and Leah. In Genesis 49:8-12, Jacob blessed Judah, saying, "The scepter shall not depart from Judah, nor the ruler's staff from between his feet." This meant that future kings of Israel would come from his family line. David, who defeated the giant Goliath and became king of Israel, came from the tribe of Judah. His son, King Solomon, ruled after him. Yeshua the Messiah was of the tribe of Judah.

Judah was part of the plan to sell his brother Joseph into slavery. He suggested that the brothers sell Joseph instead of killing him (Genesis 37:26-27). After that, Judah did not keep his promise to Tamar, his daughter-in-law. Tamar gave birth to Perez, who became an ancestor of both King David and Yeshua. During the famine, when Joseph tested his brothers in Egypt, Judah offered to take the place of his younger brother Benjamin as a slave. Whenever the Israelites traveled through the wilderness, the tribe of Judah led the way. They camped on the east side of the tabernacle, along with the tribes of Issachar and Zebulun. Judah was the largest tribe, with 74,600 men of fighting age. Later, Judah received land in the southern part of Canaan, which included the cities of Bethlehem, Hebron, and Jerusalem.

 **Answer the questions.**

1. What blessing did Jacob give to Judah in Genesis 49?

....

2. What were some important cities in Judah's land?

....

3. How did Judah show leadership in the wilderness?

....

4. Name one famous person from the tribe of Judah.

....

WHERE DID THE TRIBE OF JUDAH LIVE?

Read Joshua 15 to learn how the tribe of Judah received
its land in the southern part of the Promised Land.

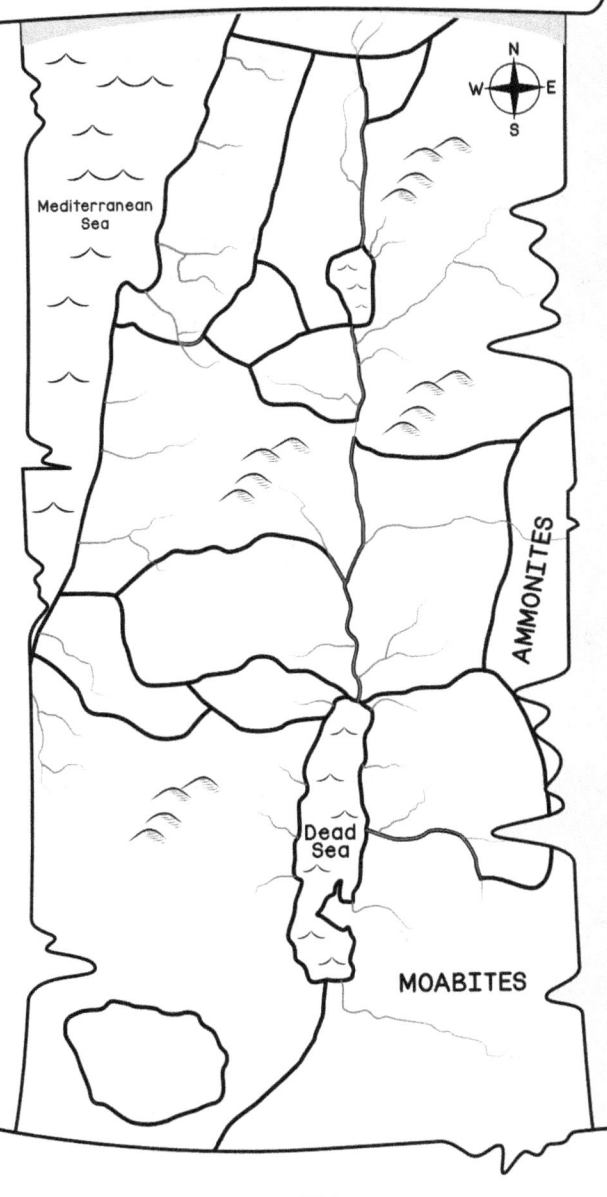

Land of Israel

Mediterranean Sea

AMMONITES

Dead Sea

MOABITES

Instructions:

1. Shade the area where the tribe of Judah lived with red.

2. Use a black marker to trace the border of Judah's territory.

3. Draw circles to mark the cities of Bethlehem, Hebron, and Jerusalem.

4. Why do you think Judah received a large piece of land?

....

....

....

....

Did You Know?

Judah offered to take Benjamin's place as a slave when Joseph tested his brothers in the land of Egypt (Genesis 44:33).

TRIBE OF DAN

 **Tribal history**

TRIBE OF DAN

The Tribe of Dan was named after Dan, the fifth son of Jacob and Bilhah (Rachel's servant). In Genesis 49:16-17, Jacob blessed Dan by saying, "Dan shall judge his people as one of the tribes of Israel." The name 'Dan' means judge, and this blessing showed that Dan's descendants would help lead or bring justice among the tribes. During the Israelites' journey in the wilderness, the tribe of Dan camped on the north side of the tabernacle, alongside the tribes of Asher and Naphtali. Dan was a large tribe, with 64,400 men of fighting age.

After entering the Promised Land, the tribe of Dan struggled to take control of their land near the Philistines. The enemy was tough, and Dan had a hard time living safely in that area. Because of this, some of the Danites moved north and captured the city of Laish, renaming it Dan (Judges 18:27-29). In the new city, they set up an idol, which was against Yah's commands. One of the most famous people from the tribe of Dan was Samson, a judge of Israel known for his great strength. He fought against the Philistines and helped protect Israel during a time of trouble.

 **Answer the questions.**

1. What blessing did Jacob give to Dan in Genesis 49?

   ....

2. What did the tribe of Dan do when they could not take their own land?

   ....

3. Who was the most famous person from the tribe of Dan?

   ....

4. What mistake did the tribe of Dan make after they moved north?

   ....

WHERE DID THE TRIBE OF DAN LIVE?

Read Joshua 19:40-48 and Judges 18 to learn how the tribe of Dan received land near the Philistines in the west, and later moved north to conquer Laish.

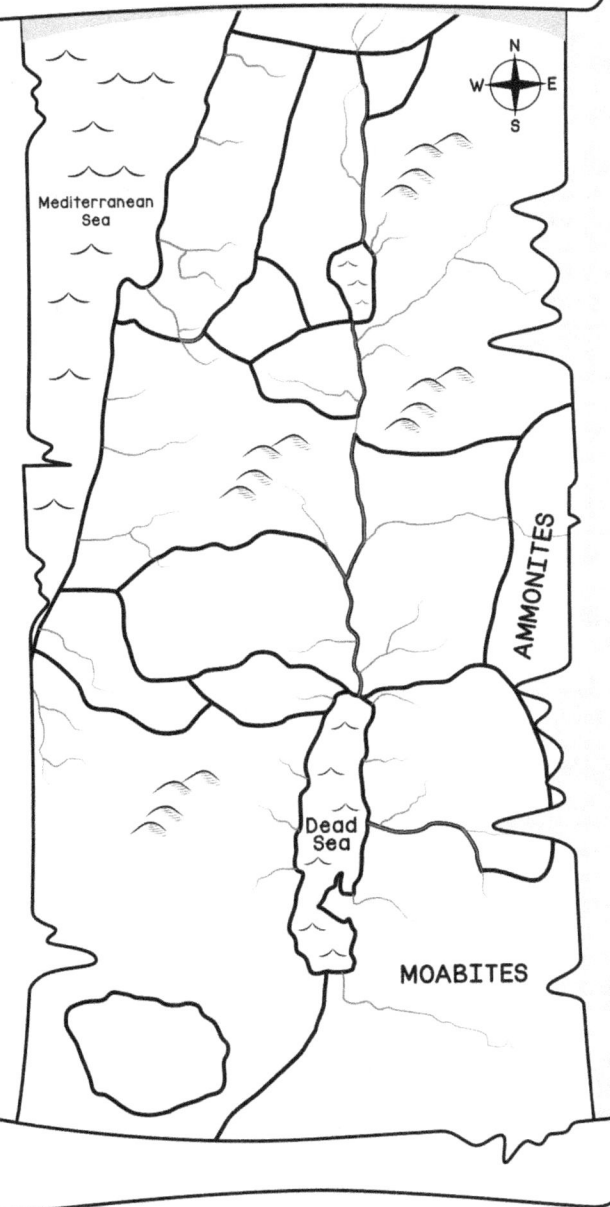

Land of Israel

Mediterranean Sea

Dead Sea

AMMONITES

MOABITES

Instructions:

1. Shade the original land of Dan with blue.

2. Use a dashed line to show the tribe's later move to the north.

3. Draw a circle to mark the city of Dan in the north.

4. Why did the tribe of Dan decided to move north?

....

....

....

....

Did You Know?

Samson's strength was connected to a special promise called a Nazirite vow. As part of this vow, he was never supposed to cut his hair (Judges 13:5).

TRIBE OF NAPHTALI

 **Tribal history**

The Tribe of Naphtali was named after Naphtali, the sixth son of Jacob and Bilhah (Rachel's servant). In Genesis 49:21, Jacob blessed Naphtali, saying, "Naphtali is a doeset free, who bears beautiful fawns." During the Israelites' journey in the wilderness, the tribe of Naphtali camped on the north side of the tabernacle, next to the tribes of Dan and Asher. They were a strong tribe with 53,400 men of fighting age.

When the Israelites entered the Promised Land, the tribe of Naphtali received land in the northern region of Canaan, near the Sea of Galilee (Joshua 19:32-39). Their land was beautiful and rich, with many hills and valleys, and became an important trade area because of its location. One of the most famous people from the tribe of Naphtali was Barak, a military leader who worked with the prophetess Deborah to defeat the army of Sisera (Judges 4:6-10). Many years later, Naphtali's land became important in the life of Yeshua. Much of His teaching and many miracles happened in cities like Capernaum and Bethsaida, which were part of Naphtali's territory (Matthew 4:13-15).

TRIBE OF NAPHTALI

 ## Answer the questions.

1. What blessing did Jacob give to Naphtali in Genesis 49?

   ....

2. Where was the tribe of Naphtali's land located?

   ....

3. Who was the famous leader from Naphtali who worked with Deborah?

   ....

4. Why is Naphtali's territory important in the life of Yeshua?

   ....

WHERE DID THE TRIBE OF NAPHTALI LIVE?

Read Joshua 19:32-39 to learn how the tribe of Naphtali
received land near the Sea of Galilee.

Land of Israel

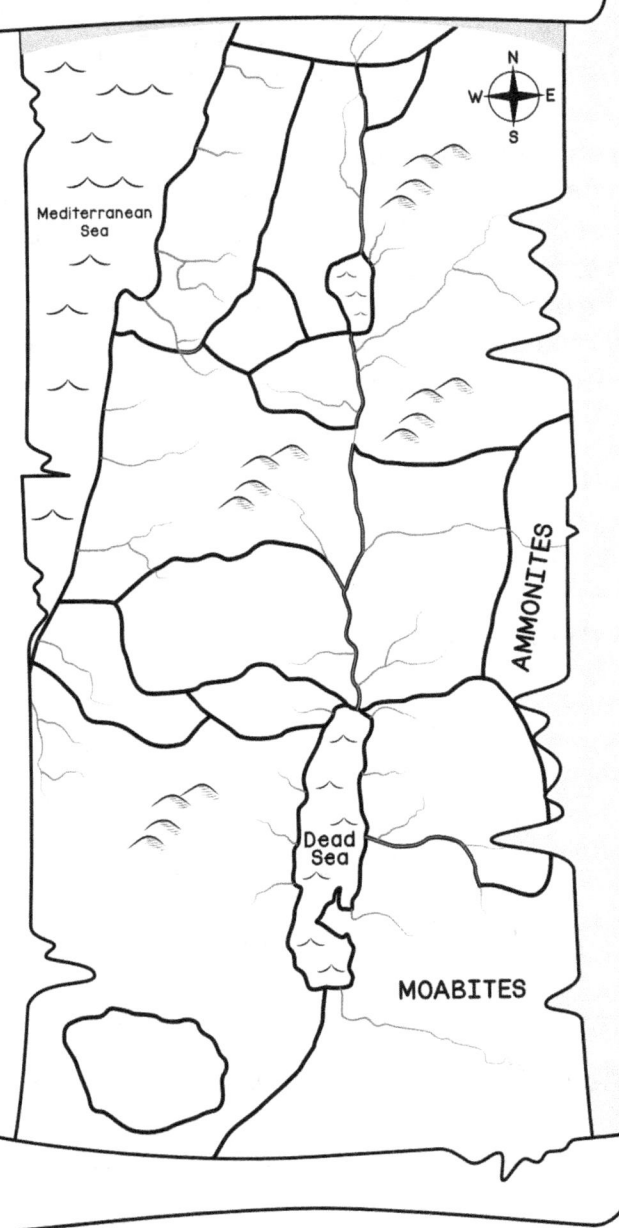

Instructions:

1. Shade the tribe of Naphtali's land with green.

2. Circle the Sea of Galilee on your map.

3. List three cities that belonged to the tribe of Naphtali near the Sea of Galilee.

....

....

4. Why do you think Yeshua spent time in the land of Naphtali?

....

....

Did You Know?

When Yeshua began His ministry, He traveled through the land of Naphtali, fulfilling Isaiah's prophecy: "The people dwelling in darkness have seen a great light" (Matthew 4:13-16; Isaiah 9:1-2).

TRIBE OF GAD

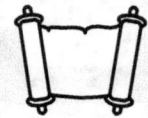

Tribal history

The Tribe of Gad was named after Gad, the seventh son of Jacob and Zilpah (Leah's servant). In Genesis 49:19, Jacob blessed Gad by saying, "Gad will be attacked by raiders, but he shall raid at their heels." This blessing showed that Gad's descendants would be strong warriors who would defend their land. During the Israelites' time in the wilderness, the tribe of Gad camped on the south side of the tabernacle, next to the tribes of Reuben and Simeon. Gad had 45,650 men of fighting age.

When the Israelites were preparing to enter the Promised Land, the tribe of Gad saw that the land east of the Jordan River was good for raising livestock. Along with the tribes of Reuben and half of Manasseh, they asked Moses for permission to live there. Moses agreed, but only if they helped the other tribes fight for their land in Canaan. After the conquest, the tribe of Gad returned home and built an altar as a witness to their faith in Yah (Joshua 22). A famous people from the tribe of Gad was Elijah the prophet, who came from the area of Gilead, where Gad lived. Elijah spoke Yah's words and performed many miracles during a time when the Israelites were worshiping false gods (also known as spiritual adultery).

Answer the questions.

1. What blessing did Jacob give to Gad in Genesis 49?

   ....

2. Where did the tribe of Gad choose to live?

   ....

3. What did Gad promise to do before settling east of the Jordan?

   ....

4. Who was the famous prophet from the land of Gilead, and what did he do?

   ....

WHERE DID THE TRIBE OF GAD LIVE?

Read Numbers 32 and Joshua 22 to learn how the tribe of Gad settled east of the Jordan River, in a region called Gilead.

Land of Israel

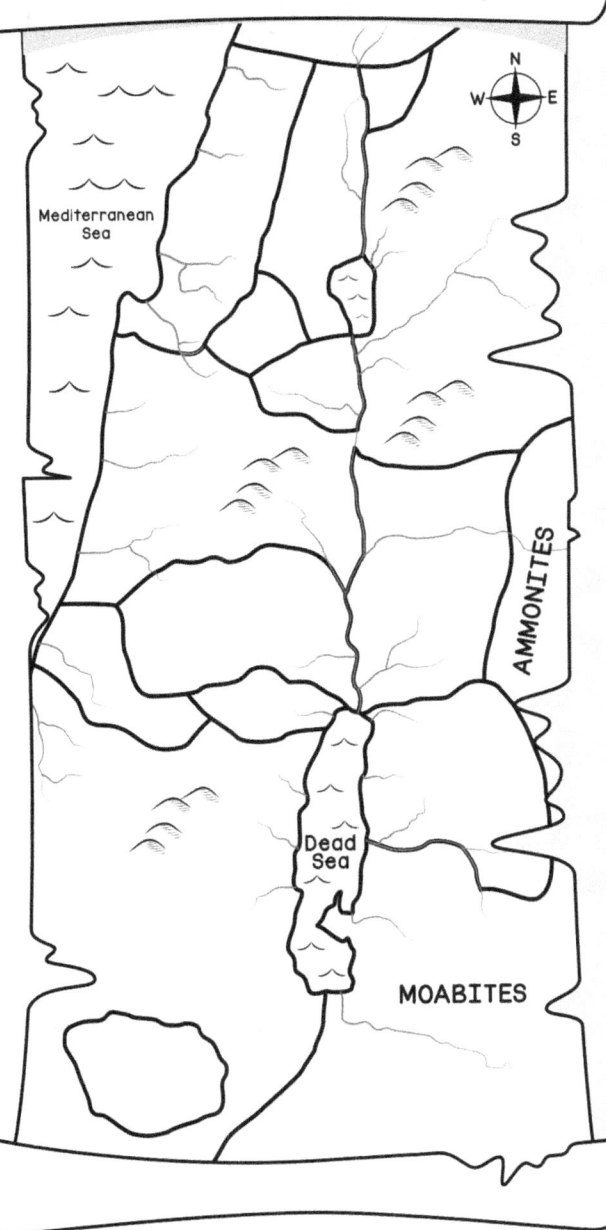

Mediterranean Sea

AMMONITES

Dead Sea

MOABITES

Instructions:

1. Shade the land of Gad east of the Jordan River with orange.

2. Mark the Jordan River with a blue line.

3. Draw a sheep or ox to show why the land was good for raising animals.

4. Why do you think the tribe of Gad built an altar before returning home?

....

....

....

Did You Know?

The prophet Elijah came from Gilead, the region where the tribe of Gad settled. He spoke Yah's words to kings and performed miracles, including calling down fire from heaven (1 Kings 17:1; 18:36-38).

TRIBE OF ASHER

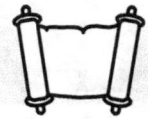 ## Tribal history

The Tribe of Asher was named after Asher, the eighth son of Jacob and Zilpah (Leah's servant). In Genesis 49:20, Jacob blessed Asher, saying, "Asher's food shall be rich, and he shall yield royal delicacies." During the Israelites' journey in the wilderness, the tribe of Asher camped on the north side of the tabernacle, alongside the tribes of Dan and Naphtali. Asher had 41,500 men of fighting age (Numbers 1:41).

When the Israelites entered the Promised Land, the tribe of Asher received land along the northwestern coast of Canaan, including parts of the fertile Galilee region (Joshua 19:24-31). Their land was known for its olive trees, wheat, and rich soil. Although Asher's warriors joined some key battles (like the one against Sisera) they did not fully drive out the Canaanites from their land. Years later, during the reign of King Hezekiah, some Israelites from the tribes of Asher, Manasseh, and Zebulun traveled to Jerusalem to honor the Passover and Feast of Unleavened Bread (2 Chronicles 30:10-15).

 ## Answer the questions.

1. What blessing did Jacob give to Asher in Genesis 49?

    ....

2. Where was the tribe of Asher's land located?

    ....

3. What made Asher's land rich and valuable?

    ....

4. Who was the prophetess from the tribe of Asher, and what did she do?

    ....

WHERE DID THE TRIBE OF ASHER LIVE?

Read Joshua 19:24–31 to learn how the tribe of Asher
received land in the coastal hills of northern Canaan.

Land of Israel

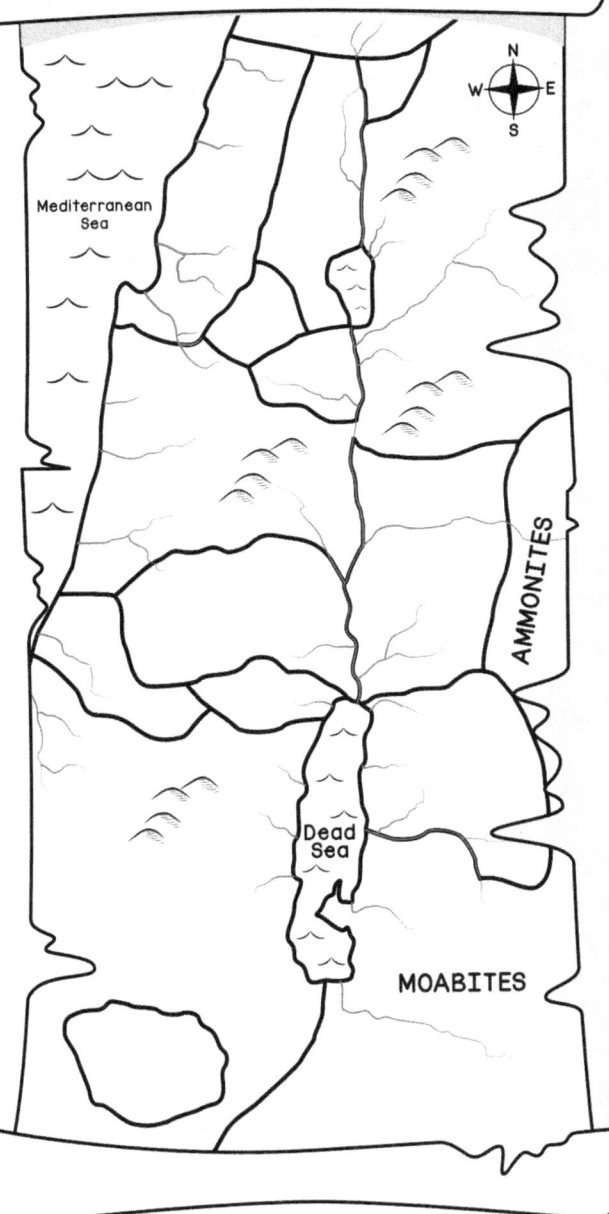

Instructions:

1. Shade the land of Asher on the northwestern coast with yellow.

2. Draw an olive branch to show the tribe's rich food and oil supply.

3. Mark the cities of Acco and Tyre on your map.

4. How do you think the tribe of Asher's location near the sea helped them?

....

....

....

....

Did You Know?

A famous Israelite from the tribe of Asher was the prophetess Anna, who lived during the time of Yeshua's birth. She worshiped at the temple in Jerusalem and gave thanks to Yah when she saw baby Yeshua (Luke 2:36–38).

TRIBE OF ISSACHAR

Tribal history

The Tribe of Issachar was named after Issachar, the ninth son of Jacob and Leah. In Genesis 49:14–15, Jacob blessed Issachar, saying, "Issachar is a strong donkey, lying down between two burdens." During the Israelites' journey in the wilderness, the tribe of Issachar camped on the east side of the tabernacle with the tribes of Judah and Zebulun. They were a large and strong tribe with 54,400 men of fighting age (Numbers 1).

When the Israelites entered the Promised Land, the tribe of Issachar received land in the Jezreel Valley, a farming region in northern Canaan (Joshua 19:17-23). Their land had fertile soil and important trade routes. One of the most famous verses about the tribe of Issachar is 1 Chronicles 12:32, where they are described as men "who understood the times and knew what Israel should do." These wise men joined King David at Hebron to support him as king over all Israel. The tribe of Issachar also helped Deborah and Barak in battle against Sisera's army (Judges 5:15).

TRIBE OF ISSACHAR

Answer the questions.

1. What blessing did Jacob give to Issachar in Genesis 49?

   ....

2. Where was the tribe of Issachar's land located?

   ....

3. Why was Issachar known for wisdom and learning?

   ....

4. How did the tribe of Issachar help Deborah and King David?

   ....

WHERE DID THE TRIBE OF ISSACHAR LIVE?

Read Joshua 19:17-23 to learn how the tribe of Issachar was given land in the Jezreel Valley.

Land of Israel

Mediterranean Sea

N
W E
S

AMMONITES

Dead Sea

MOABITES

Instructions:

1. Shade the land of Issachar in the northeastern region with brown.

2. Draw a plow or scroll to show that the tribe was known for farming and wisdom.

3. Name three tribes of Israel that surrounded the land of Issachar.

....

....

4. Why do you think Issachar was respected for both hard work and knowledge?

....

....

Did You Know?

The men of Issachar were known for their understanding of the times and gave wise advice to Israel's leaders (1 Chronicles 12:32).

TRIBE OF ZEBULUN

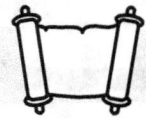 ## Tribal history

The Tribe of Zebulun was named after Zebulun, the tenth son of Jacob and the sixth son of Leah. In Genesis 49:13, Jacob blessed Zebulun, saying, "Zebulun will live by the sea and become a haven for ships." During the Israelites' journey through the wilderness, the tribe of Zebulun camped on the east side of the tabernacle, near the tribes of Judah and Issachar. They were a strong tribe with 57,400 men of fighting age (Numbers 1:31).

When the Israelites entered the Promised Land, Zebulun received land in the northern part of Canaan, between the Sea of Galilee and the Mediterranean Sea. Although their land didn't touch the sea, they were close to important trade routes and busy ports. Their land was good for farming, and the hills were great for vineyards. In Judges 4-5, they joined Deborah and Barak to fight against Sisera. In Judges 6, they helped Gideon fight the Midianites. Later, they joined David at Hebron and were praised as brave and loyal warriors. The prophet Isaiah said that Zebulun's land would see a great light (Isaiah 9:1). This came true when Yeshua began His ministry in Galilee, which was part of Zebulun's land.

 ## Answer the questions.

1. What blessing did Jacob give to Zebulun?

   ....

2. Where did the tribe of Zebulun live?

   ....

3. How did the tribe of Zebulun help David?

   ....

4. What connection does Zebulun's land have to the ministry of Yeshua?

   ....

WHERE DID THE TRIBE OF ZEBULUN LIVE?

Read Joshua 19:10-16 to learn how Zebulun was given land in the northern hills of Canaan.

Land of Israel

Mediterranean
Sea

N
W — E
S

AMMONITES

Dead
Sea

MOABITES

Instructions:

1. Shade the land of Zebulun on your map in light blue.

2. Draw a ship or anchor to show the tribe's link to trade and the sea.

3. Name three tribes that surround Zebulun's land.

4. How might Zebulun's location have helped them trade with other places?

....

....

....

....

Did You Know?

The tribe of Zebulun sent skilled warriors to support David at Hebron, but they also helped by bringing food. Relatives from Zebulun and nearby tribes brought supplies like figs, raisins, wine, oil, cattle, and sheep to feed David's army (1 Chronicles 12:38–40).

TRIBE OF BENJAMIN

 **Tribal history**

TRIBE OF BENJAMIN

The Tribe of Benjamin was named after Benjamin, the youngest son of Jacob and Rachel. In Genesis 49:27, Jacob blessed him, saying, "Benjamin is a ravenous wolf; in the morning he devours the prey, in the evening he divides the plunder." During the Israelites' journey through the wilderness, the tribe of Benjamin camped on the west side of the tabernacle, next to the tribes of Ephraim and Manasseh. When the Israelites entered the Promised Land, Benjamin's tribe received land between the tribes of Ephraim and Judah (Joshua 18:11-28). This area included important cities like Jericho, Gibeah, and part of Jerusalem. Even though their land was small, it was in a good place for trade and defense.

The tribe of Benjamin became known for their brave warriors, especially those who could sling stones with great skill. In Judges 20-21, a civil war broke out involving the tribe of Benjamin, and many of their men died. But the tribe survived and stayed part of Israel. Several famous Israelites came from the tribe of Benjamin. King Saul, Israel's first king, was a Benjaminite. The apostle Paul also belonged to this tribe, as did Mordecai, the relative of Queen Esther.

 ## Answer the questions.

1. What blessing did Jacob give to Benjamin?

   ....

2. What cities were located in Benjamin's land?

   ....

3. Name three famous people from the tribe of Benjamin.

   ....

4. Why do you think Yah chose leaders like Paul and Mordecai from the tribe of Benjamin?

   ....

WHERE DID THE TRIBE OF BENJAMIN LIVE?

Read Joshua 18:11-28 to learn how Benjamin was given land between Judah and Ephraim.

Land of Israel

Mediterranean
Sea

N
W E
S

AMMONITES

Dead
Sea

MOABITES

Instructions:

1. Shade the land of Benjamin on your map in red.

2. Draw a wolf to represent Jacob's blessing and the tribe's warrior strength.

3. Why do you think the tribe of Benjamin was known for their skilled warriors?

4. How did Benjamin's location help them support both the northern and southern tribes?

....

....

....

Did You Know?

The apostle Paul was from the tribe of Benjamin. Although he once persecuted followers of the Way, he had a life-changing encounter with Yeshua on the road to Damascus and later shared the Good News with the scattered tribes of Israel throughout Asia Minor.

TRIBE OF EPHRAIM

Tribal history

The Tribe of Ephraim was named after Ephraim, the younger son of Joseph and grandson of Jacob. In Genesis 48, Jacob blessed both Ephraim and his older brother Manasseh. But even though Ephraim was younger, Jacob gave him the greater blessing. He said that Ephraim would become a group of nations (Genesis 48:19). Later, in Genesis 49:22–26, Jacob gave Joseph's sons a blessing of fruitfulness, strength, and help from Yah.

During the wilderness journey, the tribe of Ephraim camped on the west side of the tabernacle, with Benjamin and Manasseh. When the Israelites entered the Promised Land, Ephraim received land in the central hill country of Canaan (Joshua 16:1-10). This region included the city of Shiloh, where the Tabernacle and Ark of the Covenant stayed for many years (Joshua 18:1). Joshua, who led the Israelites into the Promised Land, came from the tribe of Ephraim. Later, Jeroboam, the first king of the northern kingdom of Israel, was also from this tribe.

Answer the questions.

1. Why did Jacob bless Ephraim more than his older brother Manasseh?

   ....

2. What important cities were found in Ephraim's territory?

   ....

3. Name two famous Israelites from the tribe of Ephraim.

   ....

4. How did the tribe of Ephraim influence the history of the House of Israel?

   ....

WHERE DID THE TRIBE OF EPHRAIM LIVE?

Read Joshua 16:1-10 to learn how the tribe of Ephraim
received land in the central hill country of Canaan.

Land of Israel

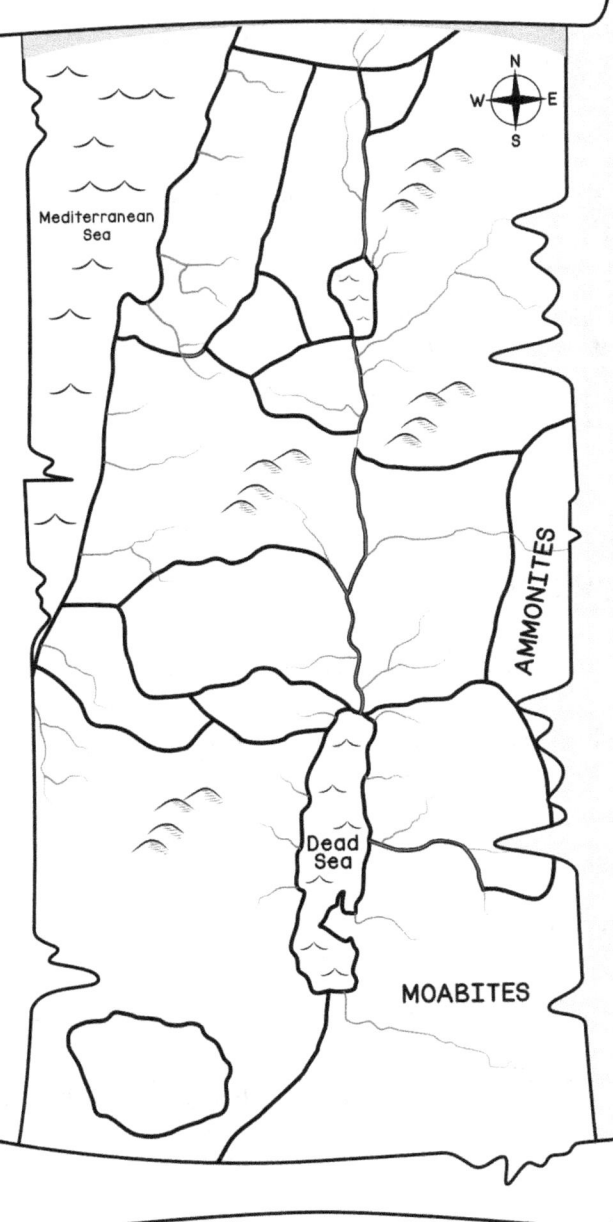

Mediterranean
Sea

N
W E
S

AMMONITES

Dead
Sea

MOABITES

Instructions:

1. Shade the land of Ephraim on your map in green.

2. Draw an ox to represent the tribe of Ephraim's strength.

3. Mark the city of Shiloh on your map.

4. Read Joshua 18:1. Why do you think the Tabernacle was placed in Ephraim's territory?

....

....

....

....

Did You Know?

Joshua was one of the twelve spies sent by Moses to explore the land of Canaan. While ten of the spies were afraid, Joshua and Caleb trusted Yah and encouraged the Israelites to enter the land (Numbers 13-14).

TRIBE OF MANASSEH

 **Tribal history**

TRIBE OF MANASSEH

The Tribe of Manasseh was named after Manasseh, the firstborn son of Joseph and grandson of Jacob. In Genesis 48, Jacob blessed Manasseh and his younger brother Ephraim. Although Manasseh was older, Jacob gave the greater blessing to Ephraim (Genesis 48:19). During the wilderness journey, the tribe of Manasseh camped on the west side of the Tabernacle, alongside Ephraim and Benjamin. When the Israelites entered the Promised Land, Manasseh received a large inheritance. Half of the tribe settled in the central hill country west of the Jordan River, while the other half chose land east of the Jordan because it was excellent for raising livestock.

One of the most famous Israelites from the tribe of Manasseh was Gideon, a judge who delivered Israel from the Midianites with only 300 men (Judges 6-8). Later, after the kingdom of Israel split in two, the northern part, where many Manassites lived, began worshipping false gods. But some people from Manasseh remained faithful. During King Hezekiah's time, he invited all tribes to come to Jerusalem for the Passover and Feast of Unleavened Bread. Even though some Israelites mocked the king's messengers, a group of men from Manasseh came to Jerusalem to honor the Feast (2 Chronicles 30:10-11).

 ## Answer the questions.

1. Why was Manasseh's land divided into two parts?

   ....

2. Why do you think some of the tribe of Manasseh chose to live east of the Jordan?

   ....

3. Name a famous judge from the tribe of Manasseh.

   ....

4. What did some men from the tribe of Manasseh do during King Hezekiah's reign?

   ....

WHERE DID THE TRIBE OF MANASSEH LIVE?

Read Joshua 17:1-18 and Numbers 32:33 to learn how the tribe of Manasseh received land on both sides of the Jordan River.

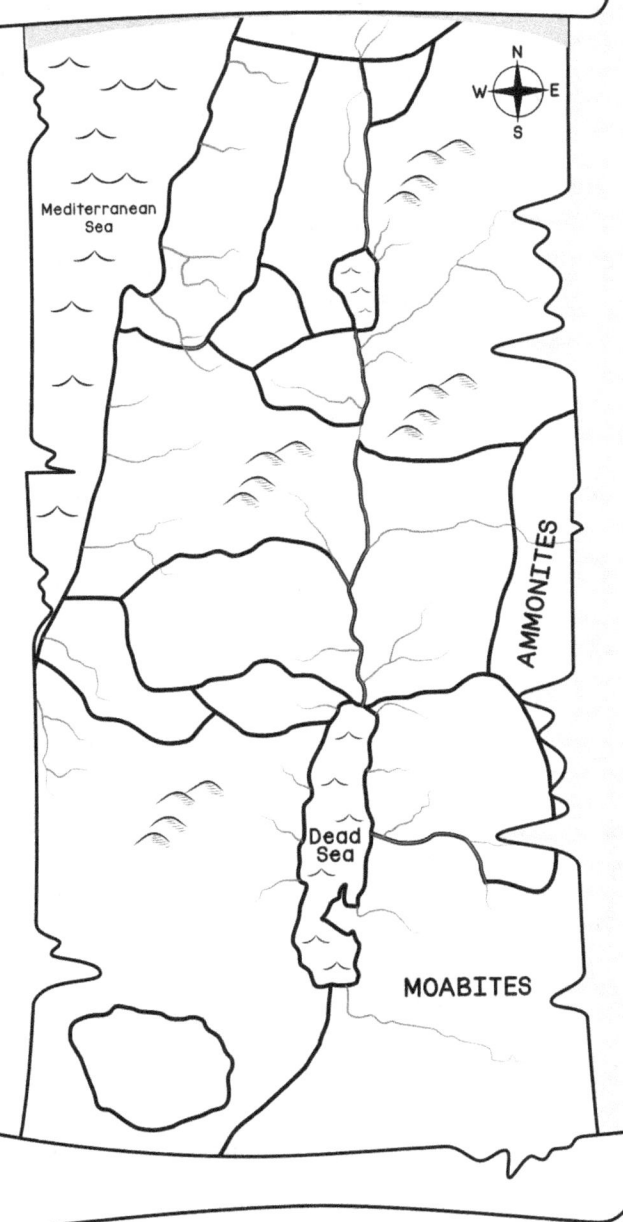

Land of Israel

Mediterranean Sea

AMMONITES

Dead Sea

MOABITES

Instructions:

1. Shade the two areas of Manasseh's land (west and east of the Jordan River) in blue.

2. Draw some arrows to represent the tribe's connection to warfare and strength.

3. Mark Mount Ebal and Mount Gerizim on your map.

4. Read Judges 6. How did Gideon respond when Yah called him to be a leader?

....

....

....

Did You Know?

Gideon, from the tribe of Manasseh, led 300 men to defeat the Midianite army. Instead of using swords, they carried shofars, clay jars, and torches. At Gideon's signal, they broke the jars, blew the shofars, and shouted loudly, causing the Midianites to flee (Judges 7:16-22).

TRIBE OF LEVI

 ## Tribal history

The Tribe of Levi was named after Levi, the third son of Jacob and Leah. In Genesis 49, Jacob spoke strongly against Levi and Simeon for their violence in Shechem, saying they would be scattered in Israel. However, Levi's descendants later showed great loyalty to Yah during the golden calf incident (Exodus 32:25-29). During the wilderness journey, the Levites camped around the Tabernacle and took care of its daily functions. Aaron and his descendants served as priests, while other Levites had different roles; guarding the Tabernacle, singing praises, and carrying holy items when the Israelites traveled.

Unlike the other tribes, Levi did not receive a large area of land in the Promised Land. Instead, they were given 48 towns scattered across the land of Israel, including the six Cities of Refuge (Numbers 35:1–8). Famous Levites include Moses and Aaron, who led the Israelites out of slavery in Egypt. Later, Ezra the scribe helped teach the Torah to the Israelites after they returned from exile. The Levites served as teachers, singers, and scribes throughout Israel's history. They played an important role in helping the Israelites repent and turn back to Yah's ways.

 ## Answer the questions.

1. Why didn't the tribe of Levi receive one large area of land like the other tribes?

   ....

2. Name two famous people from the tribe of Levi.

   ....

3. Explain to a teacher or friend how Levites served across the land of Israel.

   ....

4. Read Joshua 20 and list the six Cities of Refuge.

   ....

WHERE DID THE TRIBE OF LEVI LIVE?

Read Numbers 35:1-8 and Joshua 20-21 to learn about the cities given to the Levites.

Land of Israel

Mediterranean Sea

N
W — E
S

AMMONITES

Dead Sea

MOABITES

Instructions:

1. Draw a shofar to represent the Levites in each tribal area.

2. The Levites were given .... cities instead of their own tribal land.

3. Read Exodus 32:25-29. What did the Levites do that showed their loyalty to Yah?

4. Read Numbers 18. How were the Levites supported by the other tribes?

....

....

....

....

Did You Know?

In the land of Canaan, the Levites were not given one large territory like the other tribes. Instead, their cities were spread throughout the land of Israel so they could teach the Torah to all the tribes (Joshua 21:1-42).

Crafts & projects

Ten plagues of Egypt

How well do you know the ten plagues of Egypt? Color and cut out each card. Make two copies of each plague card so you have matching pairs. Laminate the cards to help them last longer. Mix up the cards and place them face down in rows. Take turns flipping over two cards to find a match. The player with the most matches at the end wins!

Answer Key

Worksheet: Who was Jacob?

1. Isaac was sent to Paddan-aram to take a wife (Genesis 28)
2. Angels ascended and descended a ladder that reached to heaven
3. Jacob worked for Laban
4. Jacob's twelve sons were Reuben, Simeon, Levi, Judah, Issachar, Zebulun, Gad, Asher, Dan, Naphtali, Joseph, and Benjamin
5. Ask students to answer this question. Answers may vary
6. Five words that describe Jacob: ask students to answer this question. Answers may vary

Bible word search puzzle: Jacob becomes Israel

Worksheet: Family of Jacob
LEAH: Reuben, Simeon, Levi, Judah, Issachar, Zebulun
RACHEL: Joseph and Benjamin
ZILPAH: Gad, Asher
BILHAH: Dan, Naphtali

Worksheet: Jacob's family
Reuben, Simeon, Levi, Judah, Issachar, Zebulon, Gad, Asher, Dan, Naphtali, Joseph and Benjamin

Bible quiz: Joseph the dreamer
1. Jacob lived in the land of Canaan
2. Joseph was 17 years old when he was out in the fields
3. Joseph was with the sons of Bilhah and Zilpah, who were Jacob's wives and the mothers of some of his brothers
4. Jacob loved Joseph more than his other sons because Joseph was born when Jacob was older
5. Jacob gave Joseph a special gift, a beautiful tunic with many colors

6. When Joseph's brothers saw that their father loved him more, they became jealous and angry
7. In Joseph's first dream, he saw his sheaf of grain standing upright while his brothers' sheaves gathered around and bowed down to it
8. Joseph's brothers were already jealous, and hearing about this dream made them even more angry, as they thought Joseph was saying he would rule over them
9. In Joseph's second dream, he saw the sun, the moon, and eleven stars bowing down to him, which represented his family bowing to him
10. Jacob scolded Joseph when he heard the second dream, asking if the whole family would really bow down

Worksheet: Duties of a shepherd
1. Being a shepherd was an important job because sheep provided milk, meat, and wool
2. Shepherds stayed near the sheep and used sheepfolds like stone walls or caves to keep the animals safe
3. The Egyptians were farmers and thought sheep ruined their crops and were not useful for food or sacrifices

Bible quiz: Sold into slavery
1. Joseph's brothers went to Shechem to take care of their father's sheep
2. Joseph was sent by his father, Israel (also known as Jacob), to check on his brothers
3. When Joseph arrived in Shechem, he learned that his brothers had moved on to Dothan
4. Joseph's brothers saw him coming from a distance and began plotting to harm him
5. Reuben suggested they throw Joseph into a pit instead of killing him
6. Before throwing Joseph into the pit, his brothers took off his special tunic
7. The pit that Joseph was thrown into was completely dry, with no water in it
8. Instead of killing Joseph, the brothers decided to sell him to traders who were passing by
9. The brothers received 20 pieces of silver for selling Joseph to the traders
10. The traders took Joseph to Egypt, where they sold him to Potiphar, an officer of Pharaoh

Worksheet: Match the characters
1. Trusted Joseph and made him the overseer of his house: Potiphar
2. Ran away when tempted to do something wrong: Joseph

3. Noticed that Joseph was handsome: Potiphar's wife
4. Was successful in everything he did because God was with him: Joseph
5. Got angry when he believed a lie and put someone in prison: Potiphar
6. Told a lie that caused someone else to get into trouble: Potiphar's wife
7. Blessed by God because of Joseph's presence: Potiphar
8. Was put in charge of everything, both in the house and in the field: Joseph

Worksheet: Pharaoh's dreams
1. Pharaoh's wise men could not explain the meaning of his dreams
2. The cupbearer told Pharaoh about Joseph
3. Joseph told Pharaoh to appoint overseers over the land of Egypt, and to store food for the famine

Bible word search puzzle: Pharaoh's dreams

Bible word scramble: Joseph's rise to power
signet ring, fine linen, gold chain, chariot, wife, garments, marriage, Egypt

Worksheet: Joseph stores food
1. Yah revealed through Pharaoh's dreams that seven years of famine would follow seven years of plenty
2. Joseph collected grain during the years of plenty and stored it in large quantities in cities throughout Egypt
3. When the famine began, Joseph opened the storehouses and sold grain to the Egyptians and the foreigners

Worksheet: Pharaoh's storehouses
1. 4
2. 10
3. 28
4. 53
5. 72

6. 140
7. 330
8. 400

Worksheet: The search for grain!
When Jacob learned that there was grain for sale in Egypt, he said to his sons, "Why do you look at one another?" And he said, "Behold, I have heard that there is grain for sale in Egypt. Go down and buy grain for us there, that we may live and not die." So ten of Joseph's brothers went down to buy grain in Egypt. But Jacob did not send Benjamin, Joseph's brother, with his brothers, for he feared that harm might happen to him. Thus, the sons of Israel came to buy among the others who came, for the famine was in the land of Canaan. Now Joseph was governor over the land. He was the one who sold to all the people of the land. And Joseph's brothers came and bowed themselves before him with their faces to the ground. Joseph saw his brothers and recognized them, but he treated them like strangers and spoke roughly to them. "Where do you come from?" he said. They said, "From the land of Canaan, to buy food." And Joseph recognized his brothers, but they did not recognize him. And Joseph remembered the dreams that he had dreamed of them. And he said to them, "You are spies; you have come to see the nakedness of the land." They said to him, "No, my lord, your servants have come to buy food. We are all sons of one man. We are honest men. Your servants have never been spies."

Worksheet: Donkeys on the move
1. Abraham, Balaam, King David's household, and Yeshua all owned or rode donkeys
2. Joseph sent his father donkeys loaded with the best goods of Egypt, along with ten female donkeys carrying grain, bread, and other supplies for their journey
3. Donkeys were important to the Hebrews because they were protective, strong, intelligent, and loyal work animals

Bible quiz: Spies in Egypt?
1. Joseph was 30 years old when he began working for Pharaoh, the king of Egypt
2. Joseph gathered and stored all the food during the seven years of plenty
3. Joseph stored grain to ensure that Egypt would have enough food during the seven years of famine
4. Joseph's two sons were named Manasseh, meaning "God has made me forget all my hardship and all my father's house," and Ephraim, meaning "God has made me fruitful in the land of my affliction."
5. After the seven years of plenty, seven years of famine began
6. Pharaoh told the people of Egypt to go to Joseph and do whatever he said

7. Joseph's brothers went to Egypt to buy grain because there was a famine in their land
8. Joseph recognized his brothers, but they did not recognize him. He treated them like strangers and spoke roughly to them
9. Joseph accused his brothers of being spies who had come to see the weaknesses of the land
10. Joseph's brothers found their money returned in their grain sacks, and they were afraid and confused, thinking that God was punishing them

Worksheet: Joseph tests his brothers
1. Which man's sack of food contained the silver cup?
Benjamin
2. After Joseph's official found the silver cup, how did Joseph's brother's respond? **They tore their clothes, reloaded their donkeys, and returned to the city**
3. What animal did Joseph's brothers take with them?
Donkeys
4. What did Joseph's official say to his brothers? **"Why did you repay evil for good? Don't you have the cup that my master uses to drink from and also uses to practice divination? You're wrong to have done this."**
5. At Joseph's house, which brother spoke to Joseph? What did he say? **Judah spoke to Joseph, asked him to spare Benjamin, and offered himself as a slave**

Story sequencing activity: The silver cup
1. The famine was severe, and Jacob told his sons to return to Egypt to buy more food
2. Judah reminded Jacob that they could not return without their youngest brother, Benjamin
3. Jacob reluctantly agreed to send Benjamin to Egypt
4. When the brothers arrived in Egypt, Joseph saw Benjamin and felt deep compassion for him
5. Joseph invited his brothers to a meal at his house, making them nervous because they feared they were in trouble
6. During the meal, Joseph gave Benjamin five times as much food as the others
7. Before they left, Joseph tested his brothers by hiding his silver cup in Benjamin's sack
8. The brothers were stopped and accused of stealing the cup, which was found in Benjamin's sack
9. Judah pleaded with Joseph to take him as a servant instead of Benjamin, as he couldn't bear to return without him
10. Joseph saw how much his brothers had changed and was ready to reveal who he really was

Worksheet: Joseph's secret
1. Ask students to answer this question. Answers may vary
2. God sent Joseph to the land of Egypt to preserve life
3. Joseph's two sons became the tribes of <u>Ephraim</u> and <u>Manasseh</u>

Worksheet: Did Joseph build a canal?
1. Francis Cope Whitehouse discovered the ruins of ancient dams, ditches, and aqueducts, and a canal system that paralleled the Nile River for several hundred kilometers. He found evidence that the great depression of el-Faiyum was converted in antiquity into an artificial lake from which stored water was fed to the Nile in lean years

Bible crossword puzzle: Israel moves to Egypt

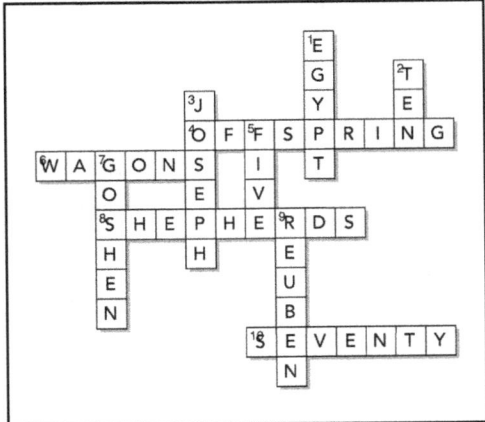

Worksheet: Decode the hieroglyphics!
1. Horses
2. Flocks
3. Herds
4. Donkeys

Worksheet: Jacob blesses his sons
1. **Reuben:** "You are my firstborn, my might, and the beginning of my strength... Unstable as water, you shall not excel, because you went up to your father's bed."
2. **Simeon and Levi:** "Simeon and Levi are brothers; instruments of cruelty are in their dwelling place... Cursed be their anger, for it is fierce; and their wrath, for it is cruel! I will divide them in Jacob and scatter them in Israel."
3. **Judah:** "Judah, you are he whom your brothers shall praise; your hand shall be on the neck of your enemies; your father's children shall bow down before you... The scepter shall not depart from Judah."
4. **Zebulun:** "Zebulun shall dwell by the haven of the sea; he shall become a haven for ships, and his border shall adjoin Sidon."
5. **Issachar:** "Issachar is a strong donkey, lying down between two burdens. He saw that rest was good, and that the land was pleasant; he bowed his shoulder to bear a burden, and became a band of slaves."
6. **Dan:** "Dan shall judge his people as one of the tribes of Israel. Dan shall be a serpent by the way, a viper by the path, that bites the horse's heels so that its rider shall fall backward."

7. **Gad:** "Gad, a troop shall tramp upon him, but he shall triumph at last."
8. **Asher:** "Bread from Asher shall be rich, and he shall yield royal dainties."
9. **Naphtali:** "Naphtali is a deer let loose; he uses beautiful words."
10. **Joseph:** "Joseph is a fruitful bough, a fruitful bough by a well; his branches run over the wall... The Almighty has blessed you with blessings of heaven above."
11. **Benjamin:** "Benjamin is a ravenous wolf; in the morning he shall devour the prey, and at night he shall divide the spoil."

Worksheet: Slavery in ancient Egypt
1. Pharaoh was worried because he thought there were too many Israelites in the land of Egypt. They might join with the Egyptians' enemies, fight against them, and escape the land
2. The Egyptians made the people of Israel work as slaves
3. Pharaoh told the Hebrew midwives to kill every newborn Hebrew boy

Worksheet: Hebrew slaves in Egypt?
1. Pharaoh wanted to punish the Hebrews because they asked to go worship God. He thought they were being lazy, so he made their work harder by telling them to find their own straw but still make the same number of bricks
2. The Egyptians didn't like shepherds because they thought taking care of sheep and animals was a low or unclean job. They had different customs and beliefs that made them look down on shepherds
3. Hebrew names found in Egypt might show that Hebrews lived there because their names would be written down in records. But we also need other clues, like old buildings or writings, to know for sure

Worksheet: Saving Baby Moses
1. Pharaoh treated the Hebrews kindly and gave them plenty of food: FALSE
2. Moses' mother hid him for three months to protect him from Pharaoh: TRUE
3. Pharaoh wanted to keep all the baby boys safe in Egypt: FALSE
4. Moses' sister, Miriam, watched to see what would happen to him after he was placed in the basket: TRUE
5. Pharaoh's daughter found Moses in a basket floating in the Nile River: TRUE
6. Moses was found by a Hebrew woman who adopted him as her son: FALSE

Bible quiz: Moses in Midian
1. Moses killed the Egyptian because he was attacking a Hebrew
2. Pharaoh was angry and tried to kill Moses

3. Moses escaped to the land of Midian
4. Moses met Jethro's daughters at a well
5. The shepherds drove Jethro's daughters away from the well
6. Jethro was pleased and invited Moses to his home
7. Moses married Zipporah
8. Moses' first son was named Gershom
9. Jethro was a priest of Midian
10. While in the wilderness, Moses took care of Jethro's sheep

Bible word scramble: Pharaoh!
Pharaoh, Moses, Aaron, staff, servants, heart, hardened, serpent

Worksheet: Ten plagues challenge
1 = blood
2 = frogs
3 = lice
4 = flies
5 = livestock
6 = boils
7 = fiery hail
8 = locusts
9 = darkness
10 = death of firstborn

Worksheet: Ten plagues, ten false gods

Ten plagues of Egypt	Egyptian false gods
Turned the Nile River into blood	Hapi
Sent frogs all over Egypt	Heqet
Sent lice to cover people and animals	Geb
Sent swarms of flies everywhere	Khepri
Made the Egyptian livestock die	Hathor
Sent boils on people and animals	Isis
Sent fiery hail from the sky	Nut
Sent locusts to eat all the crops	Osiris
Made darkness cover Egypt for three days	Ra
Struck down the firstborn in Egypt	Pharaoh

Worksheet: The first Passover
1. Moses told the elders of Israel to kill a lamb (a male, a year old), and place its blood on the doorways of their houses. That night, eat a meal of lamb, unleavened bread, and bitter herbs
2. Forever
3. Lamb, bitter herbs, and unleavened bread
4. At midnight, God struck down all the firstborn in the land of Egypt, from the firstborn of Pharaoh who sat

on his throne to the firstborn of the captive who was in the dungeon, and all the firstborn of the livestock. And Pharaoh rose up in the night, he and all his servants and all the Egyptians. And there was a great cry in Egypt, for there was not a house where someone was not dead (Exodus 12:29-32)

5. Unleavened bread (bread without yeast)

Bible word search puzzle: Feast of Unleavened Bread

Worksheet: Feast of Unleavened Bread

1. Unleavened bread is bread made without yeast, so it doesn't rise and stays flat. The Israelites made unleavened bread when they left Egypt because God told them to leave quickly. They didn't have time to let their bread rise, so they baked it without yeast
2. Ask students to answer this question. Answers may vary
3. Ask students to answer this question. Answers may vary

Bible quiz: Red Sea crossing

1. Moses led the Israelites out of Egypt
2. The Israelites took Joseph's bones with them
3. God guided the Israelites through the wilderness with a pillar of cloud by day and a pillar of fire by night
4. The Egyptian army chased after the Israelites
5. The Israelites camped by the Red Sea
6. Moses stretched out his staff over the sea, and God divided the waters
7. The Israelites crossed through the Red Sea to escape the Egyptians
8. Yah caused the waters to return and drown the Egyptians
9. The Egyptian army drowned in the sea
10. The Israelites celebrated and praised God for saving them

Bible puzzle: God provides!

1. God: 7-15-4
2. gave: 7-1-22-5

3. the: 20-8-5
4. Israelites: 9-19-18-1-5-12-9-20-5-19
5. manna: 13-1-14-14-1
6. and: 1-14-4
7. quail: 17-21-1-9-12
8. to: 20-15
9. eat: 5-1-20

Story sequencing activity: Miracles at Rephidim

1. The Israelites moved from the wilderness and camped at Rephidim, where there was no water.
2. The people argued with Moses, demanding water and questioning why he brought them out of the land of Egypt.
3. Moses asked God for help, fearing the people might stone him.
4. God told Moses to go ahead with some of the elders of Israel and take the staff he used at the Nile River.
5. At Horeb, God told Moses to strike a rock, and water flowed out for the people to drink.
6. Moses named the place Massah and Meribah because the people tested God, asking, "Is God among us or not?"
7. Then the Amalekites attacked Israel at Rephidim.
8. Moses told Joshua to gather men to fight, while he went to a hilltop with God's staff.
9. When Moses held up his hands, Israel won; when he lowered them, Amalek gained, so Aaron and Hur held his hands steady.
10. With Moses' hands raised, Joshua's men defeated Amalek, and Moses built an altar, calling it "Yahweh Is My Banner" to remember God's help.

Worksheet: Jethro's wise advice

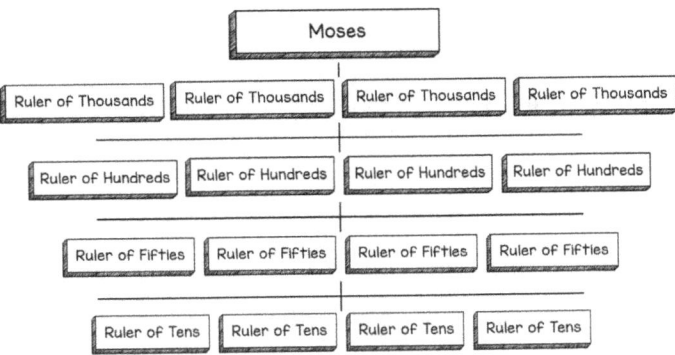

1. Moses chose leaders because judging the Israelites by himself was too hard. Choosing leaders helped him share the work
2. Moses chose trustworthy, honest men who feared Yah

Bible word search puzzle: The ten commandments

Coloring worksheet: Camp of Israel

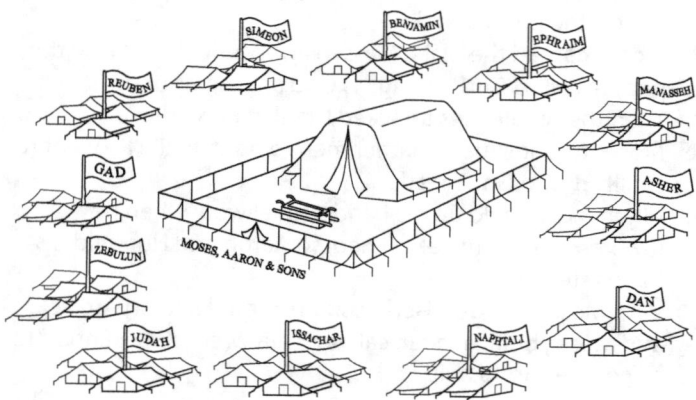

Worksheet: Unscramble the 12 tribes

Gad, Reuben, Simeon, Benjamin, Issachar, Ephraim, Judah, Dan, Naphtali, Asher, Zebulun, Manasseh

Bible crossword puzzle: The golden calf

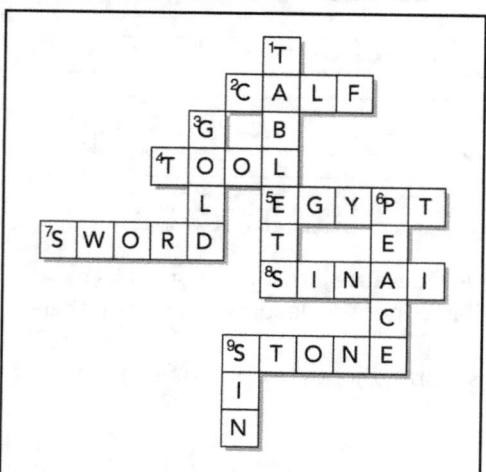

Worksheet: Waiting for Moses

1. The commandments of God, written by His own hand, were engraved on the tablets
2. Aaron let the Israelites break loose
3. God promised Abraham to make his descendants as numerous as the stars, to give them the land of Canaan, and to bless all nations through him (Genesis 12:2–3, 15:5–7)

Bible word search puzzle: The Sabbath

Worksheet: Match the Feasts!

1. **The Sabbath Day:** Yah appoints this weekly time for rest and worship
2. **The Passover meal and Unleavened Bread (Nisan 14-20):** Yah delivers the Israelites from Egypt, and they eat matzah for seven days. This Feast includes two High Sabbaths: one on Day 1 and another on Day 7
3. **First Fruits (Nisan 16-17):** Israelites celebrate the first harvest by offering the first crops to God in gratitude
4. **Pentecost (Sivan 6-7):** Israelites give thanks for the harvest 50 days after First Fruits
5. **Trumpets (Tishri 1):** Israelites blow the shofar to mark repentance, preparation, and God's kingship
6. **Atonement (Tishri 10):** Israelites fast (affliction) and repent
7. **Tabernacles (Tishri 15-21):** A wedding celebration! Israelites live in temporary shelters to remember the Israelites' journey in the wilderness
8. **Shemini Atzeret (Tishri 22):** Represents the 1000-year reign (the Millennial Reign) on earth

Bible quiz: Appointed Times of the Bible

1. The Bible says to rest and do no work on the Sabbath
2. During the Feast of Unleavened Bread, the Israelites eat matzah, a flat bread made without yeast
3. The Passover meal takes place at the start of the Feast of Unleavened Bread

4. During the first Passover, the Israelites ate roasted lamb, bitter herbs, and unleavened bread
5. On Shavuot (Pentecost), the apostles were filled with the Holy Spirit
6. The three Biblical pilgrimage festivals are Passover, Shavuot, and Sukkot
7. In Acts 27:9, Paul mentioned the Appointed Time of Yom Kippur, also called the Day of Atonement
8. A shofar is blown on Yom Teru'ah, also called the Feast of Trumpets
9. Solomon dedicated the temple during the Feast of Tabernacles (Sukkot)
10. During Sukkot, the Israelites were instructed to dwell in temporary shelters

Bible puzzle: When does Sukkot begin?
1. On: 15-14
2. the: 20-8-5
3. fifteenth: 6-9-6-20-5-5-14-20-8
4. day: 4-1-25
5. of: 15-6
6. the: 20-8-5
7. seventh: 19-5-22-5-14-20-8
8. month: 13-15-14-20-8

Bible quiz: Building the tabernacle
1. Aaron, the brother of Moses, was the first high priest of Israel
2. The tabernacle was built as a sacred place for worship and where God's presence could dwell among the Israelites
3. The mercy seat was located on top of the ark of the covenant in the Most Holy Place within the tabernacle
4. The mercy seat was made of pure gold and served as the cover for the ark of the covenant
5. Priests were chosen from the tribe of Levi
6. Bezalel and Oholiab were the two men chosen by to lead the construction of the tabernacle
7. Instructions for building the tabernacle are found in the book of Exodus, particularly chapters 25–27 and 30–40
8. Pure olive oil was used to keep the lamps of the golden menorah burning in the tabernacle
9. The brazen altar was used for offering sacrifices to God, including burnt offerings, as a way to worship and seek forgiveness for sins
10. The ark of the covenant was made from acacia wood and covered in gold

Worksheet: The tabernacle
1. For God to dwell among His people
2. Bezalel and Oholiab
3. Pure olive oil was used to light the lamps and keep them burning

4. The Israelites used the brazen altar to burn offerings and sacrifices
5. The mercy seat was on top of the ark of the covenant

Worksheet: Match the leader
1. Judah – Nahshon (offerings on Day 1)
2. Issachar – Nethanel (offerings on Day 2)
3. Zebulun – Eliab (offerings on Day 3)
4. Reuben – Elizur (offerings on Day 4)
5. Simeon – Shelumiel (offerings on Day 5)
6. Gad – Eliasaph (offerings on Day 6)
7. Ephraim – Elishama (offerings on Day 7)
8. Manasseh – Gamaliel (offerings on Day 8)
9. Benjamin – Abidan (offerings on Day 9)
10. Dan – Ahiezer (offerings on Day 10)
11. Asher – Pagiel (offerings on Day 11)
12. Naphtali – Ahira (offerings on Day 12)

Worksheet: Holy of Holies
1. "On the tenth day of this seventh month is the Day of Atonement. It shall be for you a time of holy convocation, and you shall afflict yourselves and present a food offering to Yah. And you shall not do any work on that very day, for it is a Day of Atonement, to make atonement for you before Yah. For whoever is not afflicted on that very day shall be cut off from his people. And whoever does any work on that very day, that person I will destroy from among his people. You shall not do any work. It is a statute forever throughout your generations in all your dwelling places. It shall be to you a Sabbath of solemn rest, and you shall afflict yourselves. On the ninth day of the month beginning at evening, from evening to evening shall you keep your Sabbath."
2. **Exodus 25:17:** "You shall make a mercy seat of pure gold. Two cubits and a half shall be its length, and a cubit and a half its breadth." **Exodus 25:21:** "You shall put the mercy seat on the top of the ark, and in the ark you shall put the testimony that I shall give you."

Worksheet: Ark of the Covenant
Measurements for the mercy seat:
2 ½ cubits long
1 ½ cubits wide

Measurements for the ark:
2 ½ cubits long 1 ½ cubits wide 1 ½ cubits high

The ark and poles were made of pure gold.
The ark and poles were overlaid with pure gold.
The rings, mercy seat, and cherubim were made of pure gold
There were two cherubim, four rings, and two poles.
The testimony (ten commandments) were placed inside the ark.

Bible word scramble: Aaron
Breastplate, ephod, robe, fitted tunic, turban, sash, linen, onyx stones

Worksheet: The high priest's breastplate
1. The high priest's breastplate was made of gold, blue yarn, purple yarn, scarlet yarn, and fine twisted linen
2. The chains of the breastplate were made of pure gold
3. The breastplate was square in shape
4. The names of the twelve tribes of Israel were engraved on the stones of the breastplate

Worksheet: Prussian blue
1. Prussian blue a deep blue color made from ash, blood, and cyanide from almond seeds
2. Ask students to answer this question. Answers may vary
3. The almond branch, the stone tablets, and manna were placed inside the Ark of the Covenant

Worksheet: Spies into Canaan
1. We can't fight them. They are stronger than us. - Ten spies FEAR
2. Let us choose a leader and go back to Egypt. - Israelites FEAR
3. We felt like grasshoppers next to them. - Ten spies FEAR
4. The land we explored is good. We can do it! - Joshua and Caleb FAITH
5. Yah is pleased with us, He will give us the land. - Joshua and Caleb FAITH
6. Do not fear the people of the land. - Joshua and Caleb FAITH

Worksheet: Giants in the land
1. The Nephilim were described as large and powerful people. In Genesis 6, they are mentioned as a group of mighty individuals living before the flood
2. The spies' report made the Israelites afraid and caused them to doubt Yah's promise. This delayed their entry into the land of Canaan
3. Caleb and Joshua said the land of Canaan was good, and they encouraged the Israelites to trust God because He would help them

Bible crossword puzzle: Korah rebels

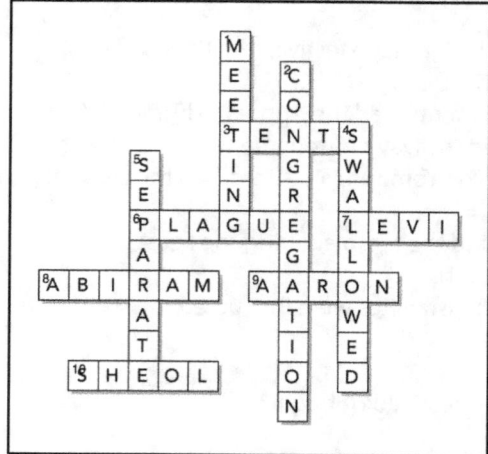

Bible quiz: Aaron's staff buds
1. "Speak to the people of Israel and get from them staffs, one for each fathers' house."
2. Each chief's name was to be written on their staff
3. Aaron's name was written on the staff for the tribe of Levi
4. Twelve staffs were brought to the tabernacle
5. Aaron's staff sprouted buds, blossomed flowers, and produced ripe almonds
6. The budding of Aaron's staff proved that God had chosen him and his family to lead the priests
7. Aaron's staff budded inside the Tabernacle, in front of the Ark of the Covenant
8. God told Moses to place Aaron's staff before the Ark of the Covenant
9. Aaron's staff was placed before the Ark of the Covenant as a reminder of Yah's authority and a warning against rebellion
10. Ask students to answer this question. Answers may vary

Worksheet: Who was Balaam?
1. Ask students to answer this question. Answers may vary
2. King Balak asked Balaam to curse the Israelites
3. The angel of God told Balaam to "Go with the men, but speak only the word that I tell you." (Numbers 22:35)
4. Balaam blessed Israel three times: Numbers 23:7-10, 23:18-24, and 24:3-9
5. Balaam told the Moabites to send the women of Moab out to the Israelites

Worksheet: Spiritual adultery
1. The Israelites committed spiritual adultery by worshiping other gods and following the false worship and traditions of other nations

2. Believers today can commit spiritual adultery by choosing to follow man-made religious traditions, rather than Yah's ways. For example, have you ever thought that Yah may see the celebration of Christmas as a form of spiritual adultery? The Christmas tree and its ornaments come from pagan traditions that were used to worship false gods. Yah even warned about this in Jeremiah: "Learn not the way of the heathen... They cut down a tree from the forest; a craftsman shapes it with his axe. They decorate it with silver and gold, and fasten it with hammer and nails so it will not move." (Jeremiah 10:3-4)

Worksheet: Rahab hides the spies
Before the men lay down, Rahab came up to them on the roof and said, "I know that God has given you the land, and that the fear of you has fallen upon us, and that all the inhabitants of the land melt away before you. We have heard how God dried up the water of the Red Sea before you when you came out of Egypt, and what you did to the two kings of the Amorites who were beyond the Jordan, to Sihon and Og, whom you devoted to destruction. As soon as we heard it, our hearts melted, and there was no spirit left in any man because of you, for Elohim your God, he is God in the heavens above and on the earth beneath. Please swear to me by the Lord that, as I have dealt kindly with you, you also will deal kindly with my father's house, and give me a sure sign that you will save alive my father and mother, my brothers and sisters, and all who belong to them, and deliver our lives from death." The men said to her, "Our life for yours even to death! If you do not tell this business of ours, then when God gives us the land we will deal kindly and faithfully with you." Then Rahab let them down by a rope through the window.

Worksheet: The Jordan River
a) Length: 223 miles (360 kilometers)
b) Starts: Slopes of Mount Hermon, on the border of Lebanon and Syria
c) Direction it flows: South (through northern Israel to the Dead sea)
d) Where it empties: Dead Sea
e) Importance of Jordan River Valley to ancient Israel: agriculture (palm and date farming, and mining of iron ore)
f) Two famous Bible stories: Joshua and the conquest of Canaan (Joshua 1-4), John the Baptist baptized Yeshua (Jesus) in the Jordan (Matthew 3)

Bible puzzle: Israel crosses the Jordan
1. The: 20-8-5
2. water: 23-1-20-5-18
3. stopped: 19-20-15-16-16-5-4
4. flowing: 6-12-15-23-9-14-7
5. and: 1-14-4

6. the: 20-8-5
7. river: 18-9-22-5-18
8. parted: 16-1-18-20-5-4

Worksheet: Battle instructions
1. The Commander told Joshua to have the Israelite warriors march around Jericho once a day for six days, with seven priests carrying shofars in front of the Ark. On the seventh day, they were to march around the city seven times, blow the shofars, and after a great shout from the Israelites, the walls would collapse
2. Ask students to answer this question. Answers may vary

Worksheet: God's Battle Plan for Jericho
Day 1: Israelite soldiers lead, priests blow shofars, and the Ark of the Covenant follows with the rear guard behind. March around the city of Jericho once in silence, then return to camp
Day 2: Same as Day 1: march once around the city in silence, then return to camp
Day 3: Follow the same order as before. March once around the city in silence, then return to camp
Day 4: Follow the same order as before. March once around the city in silence, then return to camp
Day 5: Follow the same order as before. March once around the city in silence, then return to camp
Day 6: Follow the same order as before. March once around the city in silence, then return to camp
Day 7: Follow the same order as before, but march around the city seven times. After the last time, priests blow a long blast on the shofars, the people shout, and the city wall falls down

Story sequencing activity: Battle of Jericho
1. God told Joshua, "I have given you Jericho, along with its king and mighty warriors."
2. Joshua told the priests, "Carry the Ark of the Covenant. Seven priests should carry trumpets and march in front of it."
3. Joshua told the people, "March around the city, and let the armed soldiers walk in front of the ark of the covenant."
4. On the second day, they marched around the city once and returned to their camp. They did this for six days.
5. On the seventh day, they woke up at dawn and marched around the city seven times.
6. When the people heard the sound of the shofar, they shouted loudly and the wall fell flat.
7. The men rescued Rahab and her family.
8. They destroyed everything living in Jericho – the people, cattle, sheep, and donkeys.
9. They put all the silver, gold, and bronze and iron items into the treasury of God's house.
10. At that time, Joshua made them take an oath.

Worksheet: Battle of Ai

1. A man named Achan took some of the devoted things from Jericho that were supposed to be given to Yah
2. The Israelites lost the first battle with Ai because they sinned against Yah. Achan had secretly taken items from Jericho that were set apart for Yah, breaking His command. Yah removed His protection and the Israelite army was defeated
3. Joshua set an ambush behind the city, drawing the men of Ai out to fight so the hidden Israelite soldiers could capture and burn the city
4. Yah told Joshua not to be afraid, to take all the fighting men, and to set an ambush behind the city
5. The Israelites destroyed the city of Ai, killed its king, captured its people, and burned it to the ground

Worksheet: Joshua reads the covenant

1. Ask students to answer this question. Answers may vary
2. Joshua wrote on the stones a copy of the Law of Moses
3. Blessings and curses (Deuteronomy 28):

Five Blessings:
1. You will be blessed in the city and in the country
2. Your children, crops, and livestock will be blessed
3. Your baskets and kneading bowls will be full
4. Yah will protect you from your enemies
5. Yah will bless your work and give you plenty

Five Curses:
1. You will be cursed in the city and in the country
2. Your children, crops, and livestock will not do well
3. Your baskets and kneading bowls will be empty
4. Your enemies will defeat you
5. You will face sickness, hunger, and trouble in the land

Worksheet: Gibeonites deceive the Israelites

1. The Gibeonites pretended to be travelers from a faraway country: TRUE
2. Before making a covenant with the Gibeonites, Joshua asked Yah for guidance: FALSE
3. The Israelites were told to kill the Gibeonites for their deception: FALSE
4. The Gibeonites brought fresh bread and clean clothes to trick Joshua: FALSE
5. The leaders of Israel swore an oath to let the Gibeonites live: TRUE
6. The Gibeonites became woodcutters and water carriers for the congregation and the altar of Yah: TRUE

Bible word search puzzle: The sun stands still

Bible quiz: Cities of Refuge

1. The Israelites were camped by the Jordan River in the plains of Moab near Jericho
2. God commanded the Israelites to give cities to the Levites
3. The Levites used the cities to live in and the pastures for their animals
4. The Israelites were to give 48 cities to the Levites
5. The six special cities were called cities of refuge
6. The cities of refuge were important because they were safe places for people who accidentally killed someone
7. Anyone who accidentally killed another person without intent could flee to a city of refuge
8. Someone could stay in a city of refuge until the high priest died
9. Murder was intentional harm done with hatred or a weapon, while accidental killing happened without intent to harm
10. God reminded the Israelites not to defile the land because He dwelled among them

Worksheet: Tribal inheritance

Reuben: Reuben was given land east of the Jordan, outside the Promised Land. This included Mount Nebo (where Moses viewed the Promised Land)

Gad: Gad was given land east of the Jordan, outside the Promised Land along the Jordan River

Manasseh: Manasseh was given two large portions of land; half the tribe received land east of the Jordan River. The other half received land west of the Jordan River, in the area around Mt Gerizim, Mt Ebal and the Vale of Shechem

Judah: Judah received a large portion of land south of Benjamin and Dan. It included Jerusalem, Bethlehem, Hebron and Gaza

Ephraim: Ephraim was given land in the central hill country, including Shiloh. Its territory bordered Manasseh, Dan and Benjamin

Benjamin: Benjamin received a small portion of land, just north of Jerusalem

Simeon: Simeon received the semi-arid foothills of the Negev Desert between Beersheba and Kadesh Barnea

Zebulun: Zebulun was given a small portion of land in southern Galilee, between Asher and Naphtali

Issachar: Issachar was given land in the Jezreel Valley, including Nazareth

Asher: Asher was given land along the northern coastal region of Canaan

Naphtali: Naphtali was given land in the hill country of Galilee bordering the Sea of Galilee, Zebulun, Issachar and Asher

Dan: Dan was given a small portion of land on the coastal plains of Philistia. The tribe failed to defeat the Philistines and moved to northern Canaan. There they conquered the city of Leshem (Laish), renamed it Dan, and settled there

Levi: The tribe of Levi served the House of Israel as priests. Joshua gave them 48 towns throughout the Promised Land

**6 Cities of Refuge: *Hebron, Bezer, Shechem, Kedesh, Ramoth Gilead, and Golan*

Map activity: The promised land
1 = Simeon
2 = Judah
3 = Reuben
4 = Gad
5 = Dan
6 = Asher
7 = Issachar
8 = Zebulun
9 = Naphtali
10 = Manasseh
11 = Ephraim
12 = Benjamin

Worksheet: Tribe of Reuben
1. Reuben lost his birthright because he dishonored his father by sleeping with his father's concubine
2. The tribe of Reuben lived east of the Jordan River in land that was good for raising livestock

3. When the tribe of Reuben built an altar in Joshua 22, the other tribes feared it was for idol worship, but Reuben explained it was a witness that they still served Yah
4. Ask students to answer this question. Answers may vary

Worksheet: Tribe of Simeon
1. Joseph kept Simeon in prison to test his brothers and make sure they would bring Benjamin to the land of Egypt
2. Jacob said Simeon and Levi were violent and should be scattered in Israel
3. The tribe of Simeon's land was located inside the territory of Judah
4. The tribe of Simeon helped King David by joining his army at Hebron to support him as king

Worksheet: Tribe of Judah
1. Jacob said Judah would be praised by his brothers and compared him to a lion, saying a ruler would come from this tribe
2. Important cities in Judah's land included Jerusalem, Bethlehem, and Hebron
3. Judah led the Israelites whenever they traveled through the wilderness
4. Famous people from the tribe of Judah include King David, King Solomon and Yeshua the Messiah

Worksheet: Tribe of Dan
1. Jacob said Dan would be like a snake by the road, striking at the heels of a horse
2. When the tribe of Dan could not take their land, they moved north and attacked the city of Laish
3. The most famous person from the tribe of Dan was an Israelite named Samson
4. After moving north, the tribe of Dan set up idols and turned away from worshiping Yah

Worksheet: Tribe of Naphtali
1. Jacob said Naphtali was a doe set free who bears beautiful fawns, showing grace and fruitfulness
2. The tribe of Naphtali's land was located near the Sea of Galilee
3. The famous leader from Naphtali who worked with Deborah was Barak.
4. Naphtali's land is important in the life of Yeshua because He lived and taught in this region, especially around the Sea of Galilee

Worksheet: Tribe of Gad
1. Jacob said Gad would be attacked by raiders, but he would fight back and win
2. The tribe of Gad chose to live east of the Jordan River in the land of Gilead

3. Gad promised to help the other tribes fight for the Promised Land before returning home
4. A famous prophet from the land of Gilead was Elijah, who challenged the prophets of Baal on Mount Carmel

Worksheet: Tribe of Asher
1. Jacob said Asher's food would be rich, and he would provide royal delicacies
2. The tribe of Asher's land was located in the northern part of Israel, along the Mediterranean Sea
3. Asher's land was rich and valuable because it had fertile soil, olive trees, and access to trade routes
4. The prophetess from the tribe of Asher was Anna, who praised Yah and spoke about Yeshua when He was presented at the temple

Worksheet: Tribe of Issachar
1. Jacob said Issachar was like a strong donkey lying down between two burdens
2. The tribe of Issachar's land was located in the Jezreel Valley
3. Issachar was known for wisdom and learning because its leaders understood the times and knew what the Israelites should do
4. The tribe of Issachar helped Deborah by sending men to fight in battle and supported David with wise and loyal men who joined his army

Worksheet: Tribe of Zebulun
1. Jacob said Zebulun would live by the seashore and become a haven for ships
2. The tribe of Zebulun lived in northern Israel, between the Mediterranean Sea and the Sea of Galilee
3. The tribe of Zebulun helped David by sending experienced warriors to join his army, all fully trained and loyal to support him as king of Israel
4. Zebulun's land was part of the region where Yeshua lived and taught, fulfilling prophecy about a great light shining in Galilee (Isaiah 9:1; Matthew 4:13–16)

Worksheet: Tribe of Benjamin
1. Jacob said Benjamin was a ravenous wolf, devouring his prey in the morning and dividing the plunder in the evening
2. Cities in Benjamin's land included Jerusalem, Jericho, Gibeah, and Bethel
3. Three famous people from the tribe of Benjamin were King Saul, Mordecai, and the apostle Paul
4. Ask students to answer this question. Answers may vary

Worksheet: Tribe of Ephraim
1. Jacob blessed Ephraim more than his older brother Manasseh because he said Ephraim would become greater and his descendants would become a group of nations
2. Important cities in Ephraim's territory included Shiloh, Bethel, and Shechem
3. Two famous Israelites from the tribe of Ephraim were Joshua and Jeroboam
4. The tribe of Ephraim influenced the history of the House of Israel by becoming a leading tribe in the northern kingdom, often representing all ten northern tribes.

Worksheet: Tribe of Manasseh
1. Manasseh's land was divided into two parts because half of the tribe chose to settle east of the Jordan River, while the other half received land west of the Jordan
2. Some of the tribe of Manasseh chose to live east of the Jordan River because the land was rich and fertile, and perfect for raising livestock
3. A famous judge from the tribe of Manasseh was Gideon
4. During King Hezekiah's reign, some men from the tribe of Manasseh came to Jerusalem to honor the Feast of Unleavened Bread

Worksheet: Tribe of Levi
1. Yah set the tribe of Levi apart to serve Him, so they were given towns among the other tribes instead
2. Famous people from the tribe of Levi were Moses, Aaron, and Ezra
3. The Levites worked in the Tabernacle by caring for the sacred objects, assisting the priests, and leading worship and sacrifices
4. The six cities of refuge were Kedesh, Shechem, Hebron, Bezer, Ramoth, and Golan

◈ Discover more Activity Books! ◈

Available for purchase at www.biblepathwayadventures.com

INSTANT DOWNLOAD!

Twelve Tribes of Israel (Beginners)
Moses and the Ten Plagues
The Exodus
The Life of Joseph

Battle of Jericho
The Spring Feasts
The Fall Feasts
Shemot / Exodus